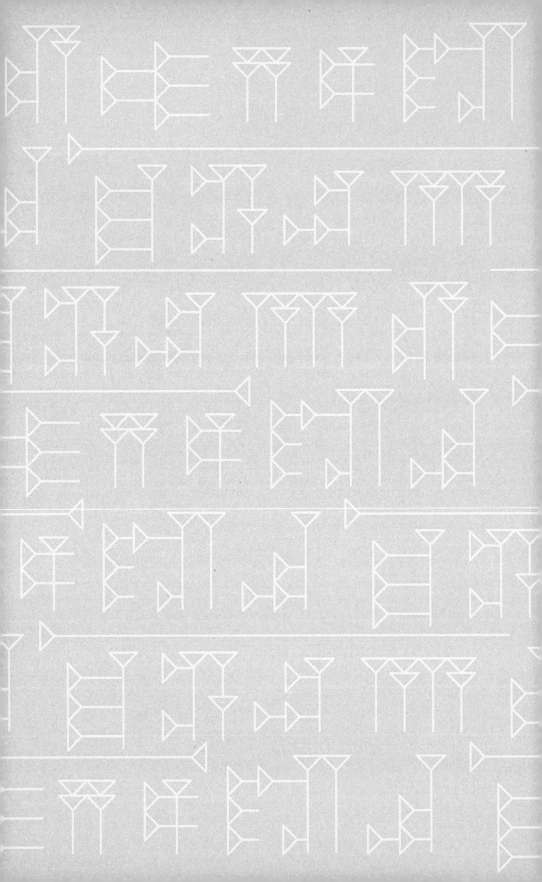

An *Irishman* in
Northern
Mesopotamia

Fish Lake Man, (aka Urfa Man); 11,600 year-old sculpture, from Göbeklitepe.

An *Irishman* in
Northern
Mesopotamia

A journey of discovery in south-east Türkiye
– a personal perspective

NICHOLAS MACKEY

UNICORN

Dedicated to the next generation
Justin and Oliver
Talia and Koray

The future is yours. May you seek out
and find your own journey.

CONTENTS

Travelling – it leaves you speechless, then turns you into a storyteller.

IBN BATTUTA

I have not told the half of what I saw for I knew I would not be believed.

MARCO POLO

This is a great moment, when you see, however distant, the goal of your wandering. The thing which has been living in your imagination suddenly becomes part of the tangible world. It matters not how many ranges, rivers or parching dusty ways may lie between you; it is yours now for ever.

FREYA STARK

The past is a foreign country: they do things differently there.

L.P. HARTLEY

FOREWORD

Since discovering Türkiye* nearly 20 years ago, my wife and I have returned on countless occasions. It's a breathtaking country with so much to offer the foreign visitor and, as a traditional holiday destination, it ticks all the boxes where sun, sea and sand are concerned. But my fascination with this part of the world bridging the two continents of Europe and Asia stems from my deep interest in a variety of fields: art, history, literature, archaeology and ideas. And Türkiye satisfies this constant curiosity of mine a hundred-fold.

In 2019, a marvellous opportunity arose to spend time in Northern Mesopotamia which is in present-day south-east Türkiye. And by the way, the word itself 'Mesopotamia' is derived from the classical Greek *Μεσοποταμία* meaning *μεσο* (between) *ποτάμια* (rivers) – i.e. between two mighty rivers of old, the Euphrates and the Tigris. Much as I'd have liked to explore the entirety of Mesopotamia, which extends into modern Iraq and Syria, these latter two countries sadly riven for many years with internal strife and a horrendous civil war respectively were sadly out of bounds.

Let me take you to another place: Dublin, Ireland; early 1960s. I was about seven or eight years of age. I remember sitting on my father's knee as he enchanted me with enthralling tales from long ago about Zeus, king of the gods who resided on Mount Olympus with a passion for hurling thunderclaps through the heavens; the remarkable feats of Alexander the Great and how he carved out a vast empire; St Paul of Tarsus and his journeys around the ancient world including Athens, Rome, Patara and Antioch; the amazing exploits of the legendary Mesopotamian hero, Gilgamesh; and there was Xerxes who lived in splendour in Babylon with its Hanging Gardens, one of the Seven Wonders of the World.

Later, I received some illustrated books about this incredible universe which left me spellbound. Then, as I got older and could read for myself, I would pester my father to bring me additional books about this faraway foreign land and I vividly recall him telling me so much about Mesopotamia and how it was known as the 'cradle of civilisation'. There wasn't a lot of money in the family during my childhood and adolescence, but I knew I was fortunate as there was always a healthy stash of books in our household. But I was hungry for more. I was so enthused with reading that I'd brave going out on cold winter evenings to borrow what I could from our local public library, and I also developed the fine art of sneaking into bookshops and browsing for hours undetected. To be free to read: how uplifting that mantra was for me throughout those early years.

As far as venturing overseas was concerned, it had to be done in my imagination, but nevertheless a fire had been lit deep in my psyche and I vowed one day I would explore these distant horizons and learn more about their story.

But there was something else at play here and it arose from being Irish. While growing up in Dublin, I became aware there was something embedded in the national consciousness which acted as a siren call to journey overseas. Prevailing social and economic conditions with their roots in a colonial past dating back 850 years had contributed to Ireland's major export: people. Emigration was an established norm where men, women and children in vast numbers over many generations upped sticks to create new lives for themselves in Britain, North America, Australasia and elsewhere. Irish chronicles recount many tales of migrations entered into under sufferance, such as the Wild Geese of the 16th and 17th centuries and of the exodus caused by the Potato Famines of the 1800s, where millions of Irish citizens sought a better future abroad.

My upbringing encouraged me, therefore, to develop a perspective that tended to look beyond Ireland's shores and instilled in me an unquenchable desire to travel: "Now, voyager, sail thou forth, to seek and find." (Walt Whitman[1]). Throughout my life subsequently I have often sought to satisfy that desire to wander. But I had to be patient until my seventh decade of existence, however, before I was able to cast eyes on Northern Mesopotamia.

And lo, accompanied by my wife and two dear friends, I embarked on a memorable journey through the streets of historic Antakya (formerly Antioch), Dara (also known as Anastasiopolis), Harran and Diyarbakir (Amida of old). I cruised along the majestic Euphrates and strolled beside the swift-flowing Tigris, both of which find mention in ancient scriptures. I marvelled at the remarkable engineering feat of the Titus Caves near Samandağ, a spectacle of human ingenuity crafted two millennia ago. Scaling the summit of Mount Nemrut, I encountered an astonishing display of larger-than-life sculpted heads fashioned in antiquity. The harmonious beauty of sacred sites like Mor Gabriel Monastery and the Kasimia Madrasa deeply moved me, and I stood in awe before the 11,600-year-old megaliths of Göbeklitepe adorned with finely drawn carvings of animals and birds suggesting rich symbolism and mythology. I visited the Zeugma Museum near Gaziantep, home to the world's largest mosaic collection where the star attraction is the Zeugma Gypsy Girl, which left me captivated. This enigmatic artwork has been compared to the *Mona Lisa,* except that the Mesopotamian mosaic predates da Vinci's masterpiece by 1,500 years. As I continued my journey, I discovered an endless array of wonders, each layer of civilisation built upon the previous, spanning countless ages in this mesmerising region.

Throughout this odyssey, my mind leapt back to the sense of amazement I had felt as a young boy when reading about Mesopotamia but now I was seeing the place for real. I was enchanted again. An arc of seeking enlightenment spanning a lifetime had somehow come together but I also recalled those people I had known over the years, no longer around, who were unable to share this experience.

This adventure stirred something deep within which released a dam-burst of energy, helping me expand my horizons of understanding a little further. In truth, I realised I had embarked on a pilgrimage which inspired me to learn more about the past and to think anew about so much.

Whilst on the move, I kept a daily journal which was entitled, *Some Shit To Remember*. My hectic note-taking became the genesis of this book which has followed in the footsteps of writers who have morphed travel writing into something extra where memoir, history, archaeology, poetry and prose, plus the exploration of ideas, all get a look in throughout the narrative.

The forerunner of this eclectic literary genre is said to be Pausanias who was born in Lydia, in what is now western Türkiye, nearly 2,000 years ago. His ten-volume magnum opus, *Description of Greece* (Ἑλλάδος Περιήγησις, English pronunciation: Ellados Periegesis) was written over the course of three decades in the 2nd century CE and has become an invaluable source of reference. Other writers who have forged their own distinctive pathways in this field are: Ibn Battuta, Evliya Çelebi, Mary Kingsley, Paul Theroux, Dervla Murphy, Orhan Pamuk, Kapka Kassabova, Manchán Magan and Teju Cole. There are many more.

My time in Northern Mesopotamia showed me this area has not only a huge wealth of history and art but also is in possession of countless ancient treasures of existence awaiting discovery.

Perhaps, once revealed, such newly unearthed treasures of existence from antiquity will enable us to become more savvy about the past while simultaneously offering insight into the future.

As an Irishman, I invite you to join me as I continue this adventure, this journey of exploration in a fascinating place illustrated with photos I took en route.

Nicholas Mackey
London, England

*Türkiye
In December 2021, the government of Turkey officially changed its name to Türkiye, stating at the time that this would 'better represent Turkish culture and values'.

ACKNOWLEDGEMENTS

A heartfelt word of immense gratitude to my dear friends, Feray and Suat, for planning and organising this adventure – all done with great panache and good humour. I treasure their friendship.

Suat and I go back a long way to the early 1980s, and it is through him and his family that I have been given a unique opportunity to embrace Türkiye: its culture, history, language, geography and cuisine. Without this cherished personal link, it is unlikely I would have ever been in a position to travel so widely in this part of the world.

A huge vote of appreciation is so well-deserved by Murad, our tour guide, who gave us new insights into the story of Mesopotamia, our driver Halil and Sami in Kalkan who put us in touch with Murad.

But above all, I cannot begin to express my infinite thanks to my wife Rashida, who makes our journey together so wonderful. Also, without her key role as editor of the initial draft I completed and subsequent versions while keeping my nose to the grindstone during the Covid years, this book might never have seen the light of day. I am eternally grateful for her positive energy, her endearing smile and her sensitive encouragement when I thought I was losing my way.

A resounding shout out for the three writing groups I've been a member of: the Original Writers' Group (led by Rupert Davies-Cooke) and Creative Writers (headed by Anne Aylor) – both based in London – and Phoenix Writers' Circle (at various times run by Tim Jenkins, Justine John and Tim Cornwall-Grant) who meet in Westhumble, Surrey. Under the encouraging, inclusive and sensitive creative direction bestowed on me from these three superb groups of writers and poets, I have learnt so much over the years. They have inspired me to seek out and find my voice as a writer.

My publisher, Unicorn Publishing Group, has been extraordinarily supportive throughout under the expert and always-approachable presence of Lucy Duckworth, publishing director and her outstanding colleagues, Imogen Palmer, copy editor; Felicity Price-Smith, book design; Antonia Reeves, marketing and publicity; Paul Hewitt, map-maker and others who made this part of the journey such a pleasure.

A final word of enormous thanks to you, Dear Reader, for taking an interest in what I've written. It means so much to me. I hope it strikes a chord encouraging you to further exploration. Onwards and upwards.

AUTHOR'S NOTE

This travelogue has its roots in the 50-page handwritten notebook (entitled *Some Shit To Remember*, a gift from my dear niece, Fatima) I kept during the entire trip undertaken by Feray, Suat, Rashida Mackey and me, Nicholas Mackey, in the ancient region of Northern Mesopotamia in what is now south-eastern Türkiye over eight days from Thursday 23rd – Friday 31st May 2019.

Woven through the memoir are verses of my poetry, along with many photos I took throughout the journey; additional pictures from other sources are duly credited.

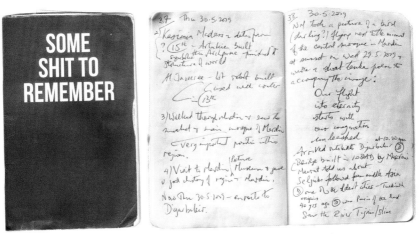

Front cover of my notebook and an extract (pp. 37-38, Thursday 30.5.2019) scribbled en route as we travelled by road from Mardin to Diyarbakir.

A note on references: a word or term with an asterisk next to it, e.g. Pergamon*, will have a corresponding explanation within or at the end of the relevant day. Where a superscript number appears in the text, this indicates that there is an endnote with a source for further reading, listed on page 243. Following this is a section entitled Further reading where sources and links connected with the devastating earthquake of 2023 are listed. The Bibliography contains all other references, websites and sources consulted and can be found on pages 244–5.

MAP OF EUROPE

N

NORTH
SEA

SWEDEN

DENMARK

Carrowkeel

IRELAND

Dublin

UNITED
KINGDOM

GERMANY

BELGIUM

CZECH

ATLANTIC
OCEAN

FRANCE

SWITZERLAND

AUSTRIA

ITALY

ADRIATIC S

SPAIN

MEDITERRANEAN SEA

ALGERIA

MAP OF NORTHERN MESOPOTAMIA

Our 8-day journey took us along the route marked in red (road) and green (air), from Kalkan to Diyarbakir.

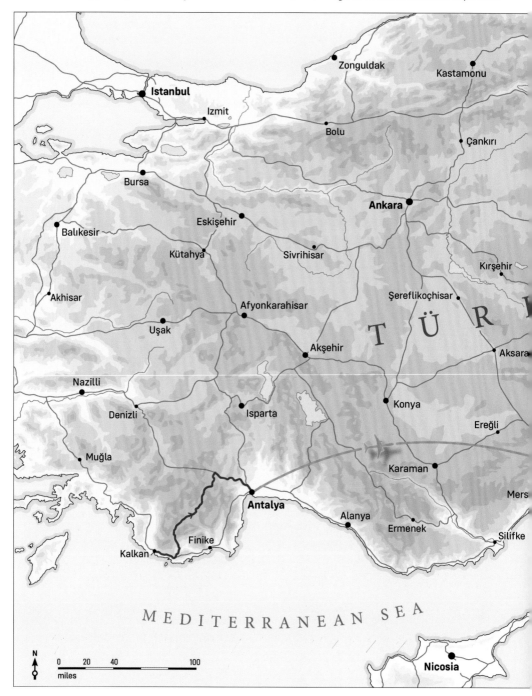

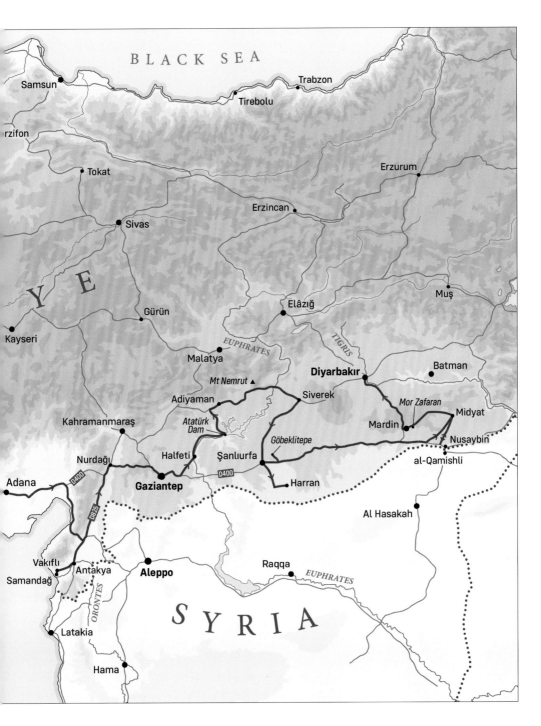

BLACK SEA

Samsun
Trabzon
Tirebolu
rzifon
Tokat
Erzurum
Erzincan
Sivas
Y E
Muş
Gürün
Elâzığ
Kayseri
EUPHRATES
TIGRIS
Malatya
Mt Nemrut ▲
Diyarbakır
Batman
Adiyaman
Siverek
Mor Zafaran
Midyat
Atatürk
Dam
Mardin
Nusaybin
Kahramanmaraş
Göbeklitepe
Nurdağı
Halfeti
Şanlıurfa
al-Qamishli
D400
D400
Adana
Harran
Gaziantep
Al Hasakah
D825
Vakıflı
Raqqa
EUPHRATES
Samandağ
Antakya
Aleppo
Latakia
S Y R I A
ORONTES
Hama

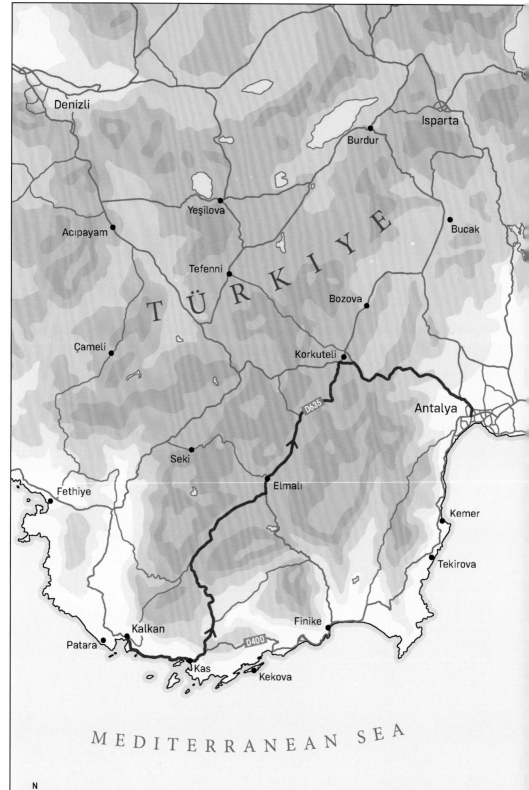

THURSDAY 23ᴿᴰ MAY 2019

The adventure begins

harmony
born of tranquillity
restoring our inner self
healing us
feeling alive

PROPOSED ITINERARY:
- Kalkan: a sanctuary to escape to
- Patara and Kekova – ancient places
- Depart Kalkan, taking the mountain road, drive to Antalya
- Arrive Antalya and check into hotel
- Explore Antalya

Kalkan – A home away from home

Kalkan, a haven of splendour and harmony, where gentle breezes bearing the scents of wild flowers drift down the hillside on their way to the wideness of the turquoise sea on the Lycian shoreline of southern Türkiye. For my wife and I, this sanctuary blessed with tranquillity and friendship serves as a Shangri-La, a welcome retreat from life's tribulations.

There's that magical moment after flying into Dalaman during daylight hours, when we are driven from the airport along a scenic highway, the D-400, past endless olive groves, fruit orchards where countless apples and pomegranates grow, vast forests covering the many hills that come down to the road, huge mountains in the far distance with villages to be seen in the intervening valleys and all bathed in that bright, uplifting Turkish sunshine. Feelings of enchantment creep back into the soul and it acts as a welcome balm from living in a cold and damp climate on the north-west corner of the European continent.

But a further thrill awaits us. Our inbound journey nearly done, when the taxi crests the hill overlooking Kalkan and the adjacent Kalamar Bay, we still gasp in childlike wonder at the sight of this place next to the amazing shininess of the sea.

If our arrival is at night, that same vision becomes a fairytale setting with a multitude of lights dotted around the welcoming hills that keep a watchful eye over this region of the Mediterranean.

Kalkan, formerly the Greek fishing village of Kalamaki, was established in the early 19th century and became a thriving centre for fisheries and trade. Following the Greco-Turkish War in 1921–22, the Greek population of Kalamaki relocated near Athens during the population exchanges between the two countries. Kalkan remained a remote spot on this part of the Turkish coastline and the only way to reach it was by use of the pathways or tracks over the mountains nearby or via the sea, as a road linking Kalkan to its near neighbours, the towns of Fethiye (to the west) and Kaş (to the east), was only constructed in the 1960s. Kalkan is fortunate in possessing three small natural harbours close by which add to the delight of this place, and has served as a bolthole for smugglers in the past and in more modern times as a low-key oasis for foreign visitors fortunate enough to have discovered it. This village has, however, become popular of late and although it retains its unique charm, there are signs Kalkan is now outgrowing its original boundaries.

Let's have a reality check here. Kalkan is in many ways a victim of its own success. Infrastructure developments often occur at speed and in dramatic fashion. The big highway that passes by Kalkan at the top of the hill was widened and resurfaced over a large area within the space of 12 months several years back. Protracted and complex planning processes, a part of life in the UK, are seemingly not a problem in Türkiye. The authorities decide on development and, hey presto, it happens. Fast. There is a lot of building, some would say overdevelopment, which has resulted in local residents grumbling about the quality of roads, rubbish collection, public amenity provision and even patchy internet services. In spite of this, Kalkan still serves as a magnet for those who regularly come back.

The centre of the old town, however, continues to appeal with its alleyways framed in bougainvillea leading to the main harbour with quaint restaurants and bars with sea views. You cannot fault the local hardworking entrepreneurs and their teams who manage to overcome the challenges they face while reinventing themselves year in, year out to provide an efficient, friendly service. Whether you're in need of a Turkish coffee, a glass of the local Efes beer or something more sustaining, such as a pide (Turkish version of pizza), mezes, koftes (meatballs), balık (fish), çoban salatası (shepherd's salad) or kebabs, you will be spoilt for choice.

If you desire a change of scenery, just outside Kalkan in the hillside wooded area further inland around the small communities of Bezirgan and Islamlar, resourceful local people are opening up small hotels and restaurants which source local, organic food, which in turn is served up as creative, mouth-watering cuisine.

If hiking is your cup of tea, then there is the Lycian Way, made famous by Briton

The gözleme chef-de-cuisine in Kalkan Market

Kate Clow in 1999, which is considered to be one of the most beautiful walking trails in the world and it passes right through Kalkan. It is 540 km (335 miles) in length and starts further west in Ovacik near Fethiye, while skirting the southern shoreline of Türkiye – sometimes called the Lycian Coast – and goes on as far as Geyikbayırı, just short of Antalya in the east.

Lycia (aka Lykia) was once a group of city states that came together in the region some 2,300 years ago to form the Lycian Federation (aka Lycian League or Lycian Confederation). For the period, this constitutional entity was a form of government with representative democracy. Patara was a thriving seaport with trade and agriculture being two cornerstones of this prosperous political coalition. Lycia reigned supreme for about 400 years until the 100s CE when it came under Roman control. In terms of geography, Lycia occupied a large chunk of the southern coast that stretched from present-day Fethiye in the west, inland up to the classical city of Kibyra (now called Gölhisar) further north and then to the east as far as contemporary Antalya, thus enclosing a triangular swathe of territory of some 10,000 square kilometres (3,860 square miles), making it a little larger in terms of size than modern Cyprus.

As you will see further on, I've added some more details about Lycia.

Kalkan has one other great advantage. If interested in the story of the past, its position is ideal for stopping off at many remarkable archaeological sites close by such as Loryma, Kaunos, Myra, Arykanda, Limyra, Sidyma, Calynda, Halicarnassus (now called Bodrum; birthplace of the historian, Herodotus), Telmessos (now known as Fethiye), Patara, Xanthos, Pinara, Letoon, Tlos and Kekova – all possessing roots going back thousands of years where an abundance of civilisations prevailed and legends abound. By the way, those 15 locations I've just mentioned, are just a mere handful of ancient sites and all within easy driving distance of Kalkan. And quite a few of these places (such as Lycia, Xanthos, Calynda, Halicarnassus and Patara) get a mention in that most prestigious of history books, *The Histories* by Herodotus.

In truth, the heritage of this region is not just classical, it's much, much older.

When you look at Türkiye as a whole, there are said to be 704 archaeological sites dotted around the country,[2] although I feel there may be many more.

And talking of driving, as you speed along the highway, you will regularly pass the eye-catching brown roadway signs which point to these sites of antiquity. But there are also such places which are not indicated, and you must then rely on local knowledge to ferret out these hidden-away locations of age-old remains: one local example is the 2,000-year-old Delikkemer Aqueduct[3] only 10.5 km (6½ miles) from Kalkan.

By way of illustration of these quoted settlements from antiquity, let's look at two of them: Patara and Kekova.

⚑ Patara

Patara is 18 km (11 miles) to the west of Kalkan and close to the Xanthos River. Patara was the capital of ancient Lycia which occupied a strategic position from about 1250 BCE until the 5th century CE. During this epoch, Patara was on the coast and it became an important seaport serving the Hellenic world, the Levant, north Africa and the western Mediterranean. Mentioned first in Hittite texts as Patar (meaning 'basket'), its commercial and political significance was such that it changed hands a number of times between competing empires.

Herodotus noted how the Lycians had the following social practice some 2,500 years ago:

> *One custom which is peculiar to them, and like nothing to be found anywhere else in the world, is that they take their names from their mothers rather than from their fathers. Suppose someone asks his neighbour who he is: he will describe himself in terms of his mother's ancestry – that is, he will list all the mothers on his mother's side.*
> *The Histories*, Book I, Chapter 173

To this day in Patara, you can see the remains of some notable age-old buildings such as the *agora* (market place), the Pharos – believed to be the world's first lighthouse, the amphitheatre, and the cistern from which the town's water was fed from a source 22.5 km (14 miles) away. The Lycians first constructed the Patara (or Delikkemer

– meaning 'the arch with the hole') aqueduct, which the Romans subsequently improved, linking this remote source inland in the hills of what is now the town of Islamlar via an ingenious reverse siphon pipeline (thus enabling water to flow uphill) over the valley in Delikkemer not far from present-day Kalkan and on to Patara. This is an amazing feat of engineering from antiquity which ensured this aqueduct could carry water from a remote source and adequately serve the needs of the population of Patara. Not only that, but the planners of this watercourse ensured that it could be easily maintained and was, to a large extent, earthquake-proof.

The head of the classical Greek god, Apollo, was unearthed in the vicinity of Patara, and it is presumed, therefore, that there may be a temple dedicated to this deity nearby, but to this day no such place of ancient worship has been discovered. This city of old boasted another connection with Apollo, as the god of the sun, music and poetry would spend the summer in Delos (an island in the Aegean near Mykonos) and would winter in Patara.

Also to be seen in Patara were a number of Lycian tombs, each with a distinctive domed roof over what appeared to be a miniature house, where the urn containing the ashes of the deceased after cremation was placed. Near the entrance of this archaeological site is the triumphal arch known as the Arch of Modestus – erected in honour of the Roman senator, who went by the catchy name of Gaius Trebonius Proculus Mettius Modestus, governor of Lycia at the apex of the 1st and 2nd centuries CE. And then there is a remarkable building to behold: the bouleuterion or council chamber. Recently restored to its former glory, the bouleuterion was built from local limestone in the 2nd century CE in the shape of a theatre accommodating up to 1,500 people where the elected delegates from the Lycian League met – reputed to be the world's first representational government. In his mammoth tome, *Geography*, Strabo* describes the Lycian League as follows:

> There are twenty-three cities that share in the vote. They come together from each city – those declared eligible – to a common council. In the same manner, they make their contributions and other services. The six largest [cities] were Xanthos, Patara, Pinara, Olympos, Myra and Tlos. … Since they were under such good government they remained free under the Romans…

Its impact down the ages was such that when the United States was establishing itself as an independent nation some 1,700 years later in or around 1776, the American constitution and the layout of the house of representatives were both influenced by the Lycian model.

Patara served as the birthplace of St Nicholas, whose generous spirit became the source of that well-known figure, Santa Claus. Other famous people who graced this neck of the woods were the military supremo, Alexander the Great, and Brutus, assassin of Julius Caesar.

Over the years, the importance of Patara waned and by the 15th century CE, it had been abandoned. During this period, the coastline gradually silted up so that today this ancient city is now over 1.5 km (1 mile) inland. Later, this ancient metropolis lay undiscovered for hundreds of years under a blanket of sand which preserved it for future generations.

Patara is not only an archaeological site, as a short walk leads you to a fine sandy beach 18 km (11 miles) long where loggerhead sea turtles find sanctuary. The area is a protected nature reserve where the reptiles come ashore in their droves to lay eggs at certain points of the year. The beautiful panorama is made complete with sand dunes, pine trees and hills in the distance.

When I think of it now, how I would have loved for my father to be by my side when strolling through Patara – as it was he who had introduced me to the wonders of the ancient world. He would have been in his element translating and bringing to life the classical writings inscribed on those Ionic and Doric columns and other stonework.

On several occasions recently, I have brought my sons to Patara and told them stories from its rich history, although being young adults, they had preferred being at the amazing beach nearby and couldn't get enough from swimming in the warm turquoise waters.

Kekova

33 km (20½ miles) to the east of Kaş, off the D-400 highway on the way to Antalya, is the coastal village of Üçağiz from where you can catch a local *gulet* (a wooden sailing vessel or schooner) that will take you to the (uninhabited) island of Kekova. On a previous visit to this lovely part of the world, as I stood on the deck of the boat and peered over the edge, I was fascinated by the buried treasures I could see lying beneath the waves. As we gently glided through the smooth turquoise sea, the sunken Lycian city of Dolchiste revealed itself – a magical sight.

The submerged ruins date back to the 4th century BCE, whereas the remains of buildings visible above water are of the (later) Byzantine period.

In the second century CE, an earthquake struck and Dolchiste partly sank beneath the waves. It was then rebuilt but subsequently abandoned because of foreign invasions which threatened the people living in the area.

Later, as we sailed back to the harbour, there were gasps of delight when we spotted sea turtles and dolphins.

Nearby is the ancient city of Simena – now called Kaleköy (meaning 'castle village' in Turkish) with a Byzantine castle on top of a hill which overlooks the area, where you can spot Lycian tombs dotted around the landscape.

Kekova is noteworthy as it clearly demonstrates how earthquakes are part and parcel of living in this part of the world since ancient times. Türkiye lies at the intersection of four tectonic plates*: Anatolian, Eurasian, African and Arabian. The unstable underlying geology dates back millions of years where dynamic tension arising from the constant shifting of these plates can vary in force from mild earth tremors to devastating earthquakes. The latter example of seismic activity can result in appalling loss of life and terrible destruction: the earthquakes of 1939 and 1999 were significant as they resulted in a very high death toll and immense damage to the regional infrastructure affected. Then, in February 2023, a terrifying series of earthquakes struck the south-east of Türkiye, resulting in an obscenely large number of people killed and widespread destruction. Further reference is made to this tragic event in the Epilogue.

Bearing in mind that Kalkan can act as a launchpad to paying a visit to other ancient locations in southern Türkiye, in early May 2019 the gang of four chums, i.e. our quartet of Feray, Suat, Rashida and I, sat down to plot our next caper. Over the years, we've had the good fortune to experience a number of amazing places around the country, such as Istanbul, Bursa, Gallipoli, Troy, Pergamon, Antalya and Cappadocia. But the prevailing mood was that something a little more adventurous was called for. A number of suggestions were mulled over but the clincher was when we realised that none of us had ever seen the Euphrates and Tigris rivers or been to the famed regions of Mesopotamia and the Fertile Crescent. So that was when we hatched a cunning plan to make a beeline for this part of south-east Türkiye later that same month. Our excitement was translated into immediate action, and suitable arrangements and bookings for travel, accommodation and transportation were completed. We were all set.

The day came when the four of us departed Kalkan on a Thursday on an eight-day trip. In true Turkish tradition, our caretaker, Sülayman, our housekeeper, Hacer and some neighbours came to wave us goodbye with big smiles, splashing water on the rear of our vehicle as we departed to wish us "Güvenli seyahatler" and "Güle, güle" (meaning "have a safe journey" and "goodbye" respectively).

A pleasant drive via Korkuteli through the high plateau (we were, after all, on the edge of the Taurus Mountains) where the clouds often float across the road you're driving along was the inland route selected in preference to the equally scenic but longer coastal route. After a two-hour picturesque drive passing highlands, the odd lake or two and huge tracts of woodland punctuated by fields planted with oilseed, pears, oranges and avocados, we arrived on the outskirts of the city of Antalya. But we faced a problem as vehicle access to the centre is restricted, so we had to make an executive decision on how to reach our hotel in the old part of town. You could say that our adventure got under way there and then, as we decided while laughing and joking that continuing on foot would be best. As we hauled our heavy wheelie baggage over uneven cobbled alleyways, my cheaper supermarket-trolley standard gear proved to be a beast to manoeuvre while Suat's superior-grade luggage permitted him to race ahead. This struggle with inanimate objects was a source of amusement for the local shopkeepers who looked on us with smiling eyes while voicing a chorus of "*merhaba*" – *merhaba* being the Turkish for "hello".

Hey ho, we'd made it safely though. We checked into the Alp Paşa, a stylish and comfortable boutique hotel which would have been the former residence of a well-to-do merchant some time past. Antalya is a favourite of ours, owing to its attractive positioning by the sea surrounded by the dramatic Taurus mountains. We re-emerged a short while later to explore the city – on foot, of course.

Antalya dates from 150 BCE and was formerly called Attaleia, named after King Attalus II of Pergamon* who founded it. It later went on to prosper as a major seafaring port under Roman rule and then, with the demise of the Roman Empire, Antalya came within the Byzantine sphere of influence. Over the next millennium, the city swapped rulers on a number of occasions between competing Islamic and Christian forces, eventually being conquered by Seljuk Turks in the early part of the 13th century CE.

Following the Seljuks, Osman I, a leader of the Turkish tribe in Anatolia, established the Ottoman Empire around 1299 CE. At its peak, the Ottoman Empire was in the ascendant over a vast swathe of territory spanning the three continents of Europe, Asia and Africa: as far north as Austria, to Iran in the east, as far west as Algeria and Spain and as far south as Yemen on the Arabian Peninsula.

Antalya remained under Ottoman control for six centuries until the end of this empire in 1922.

Some notable personages have set foot in Antalya, including St Paul of Tarsus, one of the Christian apostles who came to spread the word of God before journeying on to Antioch (now Antakya). The Roman Emperor Hadrian arrived in the year 130 CE and Hadrian's Gate was built to commemorate his stay there – that's the same much-travelled Hadrian, by the way, who had constructed Hadrian's Wall in Britain.

The renowned Moroccan explorer, Ibn Battuta, circa 1335/1340 CE passed through Antalya en route to take up a post in India. He wrote highly of the city, remarking on how well laid out it was despite being populous.

The eminent travel writer of the Ottoman Empire, Evliya Çelebi* (1611–1682/91 CE) also came to Antalya during the 1660s and 1670s. In his famous travelogue, *Seyahatname* (*Book of Travels*), he wrote that it was a "beautiful city" enjoying a "splendid climate" with "gardens of paradise" nearby where its position set between high mountains and the sea made it ideal for farming and enjoying the outdoors. Çelebi went on to say how Antalya possessed a thriving commercial area served by a harbour that conducted a brisk trade with other parts of the Mediterranean. He also observed that people with different religions and cultures were living in harmony together, so that Turks, Armenians, Greeks and Jews co-existed peacefully.

Soon after our arrival, we walked down to the harbour and we couldn't miss the impressive old city walls with well-preserved ramparts. Originally, the walls were constructed in a horseshoe shape to accommodate the local geography of the area but only segments of these fortifications remain to this day. Close by were palm trees and other lush vegetation in abundance, interspersed with colourful flowers. We passed imposing old Ottoman houses, now restored, and in use as private residences, restaurants and bars, hotels or, in one case, a school. Many of the older buildings and structures that we came across in Antalya would, I believe, have seemed familiar to the 17th-century explorer, Evliya Çelebi.

When we got within sight of the sea, we came across the Hidirlik Tower (Turkish: Hıdırlık Kulesi), a mausoleum dating back 2,000 years with Roman and Ottoman heritage.

At this point, the gods of hunger and thirst were in need of indulgence, so we stopped off at a café with a stunning vista of the bay, and gazing into the far distance we could see the outline of the snow-capped mountains. It was the ideal backdrop to dream: to dream about our forthcoming trip. We chatted over chilled drinks and some mezes, and, little by little, our conversation became spiced with the thrill of anticipation. Very early the next day, we were due to fly from Antalya further east to Adana where we were to meet our tour guide, Murad, to explore Northern Mesopotamia.

We were on a mission.

The evening gently rolled over us as we walked by many attractive places to eat and drink in the open air, where groups playing different types of music added to the atmosphere in these pleasant surroundings. In truth, we were spoilt for choice. After dinner we made our way to several venues where there was live music. You might say the four chums had been enjoying a bar crawl, ending up just outside our hotel where we stopped for a night cap listening to a jazz duo. It was the perfect way to end a perfect day.

*Strabo

64/63 BCE–24 CE; a Greek philosopher, historian and geographer, born in Amaseia (modern-day Amasya) in the Black Sea region of contemporary Türkiye, who wrote the seminal book, *Geography*, which gives a comprehensive account of the ancient world as known to the Greeks and Romans. *Geography* is composed of 17 books and one of the highlights is the extensive use of maps with distances shown in the most precise way then known. *Geography* was considered a pioneering work of learning in the fields of cartography and geography.

*Tectonic plates

Geologists have defined that the Earth's crust (aka the lithosphere) is made up of a number of large plates (called tectonic plates) that piece together like a jigsaw along fault lines. Due to a global process known as continental drift which has been in operation for millions of years, these tectonic plates are in constant motion along these fault lines. Depending on the degree of movement of these plates in relation to each other, earth tremors or earthquakes can result.

*Pergamon

The remains of this ancient city are to be found in present day Izmir Province in the west of Türkiye. Pergamon was reputed to have the second largest library of the classical era after Alexandria, Egypt.

*Evliya Çelebi

Born in Istanbul to a wealthy family in 1611 CE where scholarship was highly valued. His birth name was Dervis Mehmed Zilli and through childhood study and memorisation of the Qur'an, he was awarded the honorary title of *Evliya Çelebi*, which translates into English as 'holy nobleman' or 'gentleman'.

Evliya started his life as a traveller when still a young man and travelled extensively in the Ottoman Empire and beyond, including Russia, Iran and central Asia. His magnum opus, *Seyahatname* (*Book of Travels*) is a ten-volume masterpiece of Ottoman travel literature which is a wide-ranging description of the many places he visited, the people he encountered and the cultures he came across. Çelebi possessed a unique writing style which was descriptive, engaging and richly infused with historical and cultural details. Using at times poetic, humorous and vibrant language, he was able to give the reader a vivid insight into the sights, smells and sounds of the many places he went to and the experiences he had. It is a delight to read but should be studied with a pinch of salt as some descriptions of events and places are a bit too fantastic. His date and place of death are uncertain: depending on what sources are consulted, his demise could have occurred as early as 1682 or as late as 1691 and it is also unclear if he died in Cairo or Istanbul.

Although the work and writings of Çelebi had been known to scholars for many years, his travelogue *Seyahatname* was not published until 1838 in Istanbul – about 150 years after his death. It is estimated that this tome runs to 10,000 pages of Ottoman Turkish and has not yet been entirely translated into English. Further references to Evliya Çelebi are to be seen on Days 3, 5 and 8.

Kalkan.

Kalamar Bay, Kalkan.

Open space is becoming a premium in Kalkan.

Main Street, Patara.

Commemorative tablet in classical Greek mentioning Tiberius, Patara.

Patara amphitheatre.

Arch of Modestus, Patara.

Replica of an ancient sailing vessel, Patara.

Patara Beach, at sunset.

Kaş.

Kaş Harbour.

Kaş.

Amphitheatre, Xanthos.

Aqueduct at Delikkemer, dating back to the Lycians and the Romans.

Passageway beneath the Delikkemer Aqueduct.

Agora, Tlos.

Necropoli, Tlos.

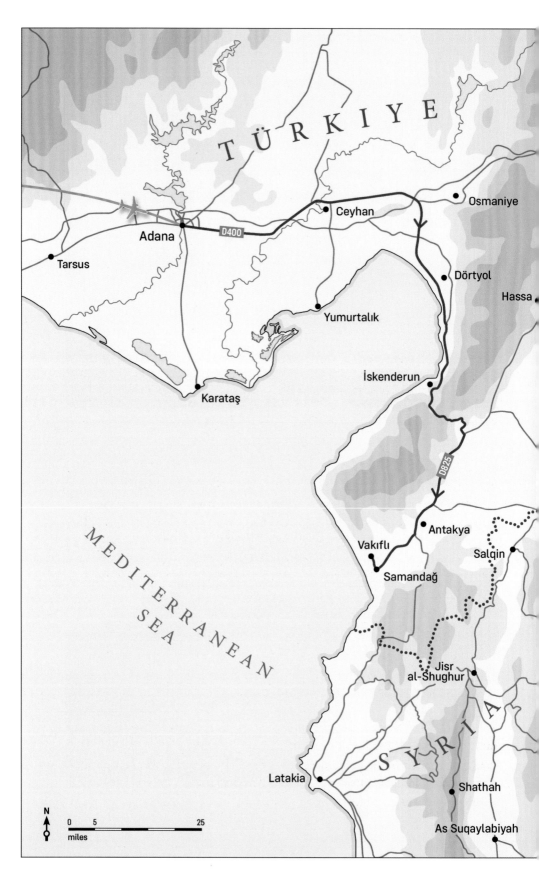

FRIDAY 24TH MAY 2019

Where hearts are open for new experiences

an open mind is the key
when embarking
on a journey
of discovery
and rediscovery

PROPOSED ITINERARY:
▷ Fly from Antalya to Adana
▷ Meet tour guide
▷ Onwards to Antakya

At dawn, we set off from the hotel to catch a plane from Antalya to Adana. On this very early morning flight, Turkish Airlines provided us with a fortifying breakfast served by a friendly cabin crew. That really buoyed us up and on arrival at Adana airport we were cheerfully greeted by our tour guide, Murad, and Halil, the driver, who were going to spend the next seven days with us.

Adana

I stayed fifteen days in Coa [former name of Adana], *a great and populous city, where the most learned, the most devout, the most noble, and the most wealthy people of the Province of Halab* [Aleppo] *are to be found.*

Evliya Çelebi, *Seyahatname* [*The Book of Travels*] 1671–72

Some brief observations about present-day Adana: an urban area even larger than Antalya with nearly 2 million people. It is inland about 35 km (22 miles) from the coast, on the River Seyhan and set in a rich agricultural region. This city has origins that go back a long way with a reference in the Bible under the name of 'Coa'.

After introductions and the stowage of our baggage in a black, six-seater MPV driven by Halil, we set off for Antakya via İskenderun – a journey of 200 km (125 miles). The weather was sunny and warm and, thankfully, there was an ample supply of drinking water available. As we wended our way out of Adana, Murad began to talk in captivating tones of the proposed schedule we were going to follow as he mentioned many things: the names of places such as Gaziantep, the rivers Tigris and Euphrates, Midiyat, Diyarbakir; the archaeological sites of Harran, Göbeklitepe, Mount Nemrut and Dara; historical figures such as Alexander the Great, Saladin, Seleucus, St Peter, Zaleeha and many more; monasteries; mosques; the varied legends; the types of different food we'd savour.

Wow! With this heady mix of places and such a multitude of things to absorb in one fell swoop, my mind, I must confess, was a tad giddy at this point. The significance of our travels began to take root and that there would be a lot to absorb, especially as my ear had picked up on a few places I had never even heard of. A thought popped into my brain; was this going to be a journey in more ways than anticipated?

☦ The road sign to Tarsus – pointing to something old and something new

Further along the well-paved Turkish highway leading out of Adana, we spotted a big sign pointing to Tarsus. Tarsus: in an instant, that single word with its connotation of the divine catapulted me back to my 14-year-old self when I attended Sunday School back in Dublin, 1969. Never did I think that one day, some 50+ years later, I would actually pass within a stone's throw of Tarsus, a town associated with St Paul. I mentioned my childhood memory about religious studies and Suat pondered aloud about this saintly figure and his letters to the Corinthians. This provoked a discussion amongst us about St Paul and why he had felt it necessary not only to engage in correspondence with the Christian community in the ancient Greek city of Corinth, a thriving commercial hub nearly 2,000 years ago, but also to make haste to the place on a number of occasions. History tells us that his pastoral visits and his letters (also known as epistles) were written to correct what St Paul saw as misguided interpretations of the holy word urging uniformity of belief among the Christians, "that ye all speak the same thing and that there be no divisions among you".

Rashida reminded me when, as a hard-up young couple, we had been to Corinth in December 1980. We had hitchhiked from Thessaloniki in the north of Greece to the Peloponnese in the far south of the country. We then sailed through the Corinth Canal, arriving at the ruined metropolis of Κόρινθος (pronounced Korinthos). Two things I remember about that trip of over 40 years ago: firstly, how we only saw children and elderly people and were told that most of the adults had migrated to the capital, elsewhere in Greece or overseas for studies or employment. Secondly,

I could recall tales of the classical world my father had told me back in Ireland as a child where Athens, Sparta and, of course, Corinth, among others, had been writ large in my youthful universe.

So, in our mid-20s and then again in our 60s, Rashida and I had had the good fortune to delight in this memorable part of Greece twice.

Aboard our minivan heading to İskenderun, the four of us continued on our journey eastwards. Everyone, including Murad, had enthusiastically chipped in with their understanding of what history meant to them, so these exchanges revealed how each one of us had a different 'take' on the subject matter we were eager to share. This set an exciting tone for what lay in store for us on our journey of exploration over the next six days, as our conversations became peppered with the new knowledge we were assimilating. With this interest in the past uppermost in our minds, one could be irreverent and adopt the British playwright, Alan Bennett's definition: "History is just one f*cking thing after another." Or, one could take a different path and delve deeper into this fascinating subject which arises from the classical Greek word, ιςτορία (*istoria*) meaning 'inquiry'. This origin gets to the heart of the matter: an examination of the past. But it goes further – and I learnt this from my father, a history graduate of Trinity College Dublin – such an analysis of events, ideas and phenomena from times previous should be undertaken without prejudice. History should focus, therefore, on the truth arising from the past and how it illuminates our present understanding of a former period, while in turn offering an insight into the future. Thus, an arc of awareness embracing the past, present and future can be gained from history.

And so, on Day 2 of our North Mesopotamian journey, it was becoming clear to us that there was going to be a lot to learn. The quartet was energised.

İskenderun - the Russians have landed

Scanderoon lies in the latitude of 34 or very little more. The town is very inconsiderable. It hath in it three factories, which are all the grace of the town: the English factory exceeding that of the French as much as doth the Venetians.
From the diary of Reverend Henry Teonge, a Royal Navy chaplain, who voyaged to this part of the world in the 1670s and wrote an account of his travels, including that of a journey on horseback from İskenderun to Aleppo in modern-day Syria – a distance of 110 km (70 miles).

And now, in 2019, our road journey was just under three hours as we followed the main route of the E91 until İskenderun, which we drove past noting its importance as a commercial city on the coast where the manufacture of iron and steel is carried out.

We saw many large industrial plants in operation built by the Russians and where more than 20,000 people are employed. Large clouds of smoke were seen belching out from hefty-looking, tall chimneys that must be a concern for ecologists.

İskenderun was originally called Alexandretta after its founder, Alexander the Great, 2,300 years ago, who had been through here during his military campaigns. During the course of his rule, the Macedonian king and army leader went on to name some 70 cities and settlements throughout his enormous empire, which stretched from modern-day Albania in the west as far as Afghanistan in the east.

Antakya – with a delightful free and easy air about it

Antakya is a beautiful city, situated on the banks of the River Asi*. It is surrounded by gardens and orchards and is a place of great beauty and charm.

Evliya Çelebi, *Seyahatname* [*The Book of Travels*], 1655

Leaving İskenderun behind us, we took the D-817 and D-825 highway routes, threading our way inland until our eventual arrival in Antakya (formerly Antioch). Our stylish vehicle went as far as it could go, meandering through the winding streets of the oldest part of this ancient city, until they became too narrow and unevenly paved to proceed. We disembarked and decided to continue on foot, lugging our bags to our hotel as we had done in Antalya the previous day. History was repeating itself! We were, however, in excellent spirits and as usual in these circumstances, Suat surged on ahead and we followed in his wake with Feray and Rashida somewhere in the middle and I being tail-end Charlie. Out of the blue, two local lads appeared and gently took hold of the cases that Rashida and Feray were labouring with and they walked on confidently behind Suat. Not a word was exchanged until the two young men deposited the heavy cases with a smile at the entrance of our hotel, the Jasmine Konak. We stood in amazement at how this duo of good Samaritans had helped us and before we could even react and offer them recompense for their good deed, these amazingly helpful teenagers had already turned around and were walking away. As they did so, we called out our grateful "*çok teşekkür ederim*" (Turkish for 'thank you very much').

We were warmly greeted by Huda, the daughter of the hotel owner, Mr Yilmaz. Huda spoke excellent English and both she and her father made us feel very welcome while we drank freshly made lemonade in the shade of a pomegranate tree next to a fountain. Our thirst quenched, Murad suggested lunch elsewhere in Antakya.

Led by our swift-moving tour guide through busy streets, we set off on foot to another part of town where we were promised a local delicacy: the famous tepsi kebab.

We learnt that Antakya is the capital of Hatay Province in a region of Türkiye bordered on the west by the Mediterranean and to the south and east by Syria, whose frontier is marked out by the Orontes River only 16 km (10 miles) away.

In ancient times, it was known as Antioch and, for centuries, it was one of the largest cities of the Roman Empire. Although archaeological evidence suggests that the area has been occupied for more than 6,000 years, Antioch was brought into being in 300 BCE by the Hellenistic king, Seleucus I, after the death of Alexander the Great. It went on to play a vital function in the Seleucid kingdom within the Roman Empire. As a city, it served important roles at key periods of history: during the early years of Christianity with the establishment of the Syriac Orthodox Church, the advent of Islam in the 7th century and from the 10th century with the Crusades.

Antakya has had a long, and, on occasions, turbulent history as it changed hands at various periods when the Crusades and Islam were in conflict and recently, in the 20th century, it enjoyed independence briefly as a sovereign nation from 1938–39 before being absorbed into Türkiye. It is now home to 250,000 people drawn from differing ethnic and religious backgrounds.

We saw a number of local landmarks, including the city market and, at one point, our guide paused at a large place of worship, the Habibi Neccar Mosque which is reportedly the oldest mosque in Anatolia, formerly a church and before that a pagan temple. Two Christian saints are interred in this mosque, believed to be Jonah and John the Baptist. It was the time of *Dhuhr* (the noon prayer) and being the month of Ramadan, many worshippers were entering the mosque. This is where an elderly gentleman, in pendulous white flowing robes, embraced me as a long-lost brother. This was perfect fodder for Suat who quipped, "Welcome to the brotherhood, Nicholas, and you know, of course, why he embraced you?" I shook my head, wondering where this line of thought was heading and Suat, warming to his theme, proclaimed, "Because you are a perfect subject for conversion."

We continued with our stroll through Antakya in search of the lunch we had been promised, as by this stage we were truly famished.

Eventually, we reached our objective, a butcher's shop (called Sağıroğlu Et Pazari, meaning Sağıroğlu [name of the proprietor] Meat Market) on the main thoroughfare.

We entered and were greeted by the shop staff. Various cuts of meat were on display and the place was spotlessly clean. I spotted sawdust on the floor – that took me back to another place: to the butcher's on Lower Baggot Street in Dublin on those many errands as a child for my mother and the sawdust always on the floor, that pungent aroma of freshly butchered meat I'll never forget and the cheery faces of those I dealt with more than 50 years ago. I even knew the people who served me by name, they knew mine and the butcher's shop was also familiar with my mother's favourite cuts of meat – echoes of a Dublin childhood.

Back to the present and once inside this Antakyan establishment we were made to feel at home by Orhan, the owner, and his family. We were shown through to a small restaurant at the back and served a mouth-watering lunch that seemed to find new senses of delight in our taste buds: the tepsi kebab was most definitely worth the trek downtown alright and we cleared our plates. We were also pleasantly surprised how reasonably priced this meal was.

Tepsi kebab is an Antakyan speciality made from very finely chopped minced lamb with added onions, tomatoes, peppers, garlic and parsley. Orhan and family, we were given to understand, enjoy an excellent reputation for this dish. 'Tepsi' is the Turkish word for tray and the meal is served traditionally on a flat round dish.

As we ate, Murad regaled us with local folklore and drew our attention to some old photos on the wall.

Murad, our exceptional tour guide

Looking at these pictures, the conversation touched on many aspects of life in this part of Türkiye and how it is closely linked to the neighbouring country of Syria. The image of the Aleppo *noria* (water wheel) caught our eye and our host informed us that it was situated on the banks of the Orontes River in the Syrian city of Aleppo – some 97 km (60 miles) distant. Historically, this *noria* became a symbol of Aleppo and was part of an ancient irrigation system carrying water from the river.

Memory took a hold once again as I was whisked back to an Ireland of the early 1960s and those enchanting walks my father took me on as a very small boy at weekends when we explored the River Dodder and nearby haunts, close to where we lived in Clonskeagh to the south of Dublin. Along our route, there was an ancient water mill overlooking the river that appeared to my childish perspective like a large lake where swans, geese and ducks glided over the watery domain. This Dodder mill was smaller than its Syrian counterpart, but I do recall its endless circular motion as it rotated and the water tumbling from the vanes as it completed each turning cycle.

Fast forward to the Antakyan restaurant and our scrumptious local fare where we enjoyed a dessert of baklava and another dish served with tahini (made from toasted ground sesame) accompanied by black tea typically served in small glasses. The genuine warmth and friendship shown to us left an indelible impression. I picked up that Murad was making constant reference to *Mesopotamia* and the *Fertile Crescent* in relation to our tour and one got the sense that a clear understanding of these terms would be helpful. So, what are they?

⚹ Fertile Crescent

As its name implies, this part of the world is endowed with fertile, well-watered soils occupying a crescent-shaped region in the Middle East spanning modern-day Iraq, Israel, Palestine, Syria, Lebanon, Egypt and Jordan, as well as the south-eastern part of Türkiye and the western fringes of Iran, with Cyprus included.

The area has been called the 'cradle of civilisation'* because it is where settled farming first began to emerge as people started the process of clearance and modification of natural vegetation in order to grow crops.

⚹ Mesopotamia

The word 'Mesopotamia' is from the ancient Greek, Μεσοποταμία ('Meso' meaning in the middle of or between and 'potamia' meaning rivers).

In his monumental and complex study of the ancient world, *The Histories*, dating from the 5th century BCE, Herodotus wrote of Mesopotamia:

> *For Babylonian territory is completely criss-crossed by canals, just as Egypt is.*
> *The largest of these canals, which is navigable, tends south-east and leads from the*
> *Euphrates to another river, the Tigris, on which the city of Ninus was built. … and*
> *when the soil is exceptionally fertile, the yield can increase to 300 times the weight*
> *of the seed grain. … Palm trees grow all over the plain and the majority of them*
> *produce fruit, which people use to make food, wine and syrup.*
> *The Histories*, Book 1, Chapters 176–184 and 193; Book 3, Chapters 150–153

When viewed from a contemporary perspective, Mesopotamia is an historical part of Western Asia situated within the Tigris-Euphrates river system, in the northern part of the Fertile Crescent. It approximately covers modern-day Iraq, Kuwait, the eastern parts of Syria, south-eastern Türkiye, and land along the Turkish-Syrian and Iran-Iraq borders.

With no axes to grind on my part as author, it is fascinating to note that although Herodotus was writing some 2,400 years ago, his observations on Mesopotamia, its people, its bountiful agricultural lands and its complex politics can still be seen to ring true today.

Geology

Since we're talking about the geography of this part of the world, let's spend a moment or two looking at what's underfoot when we walked about the place in Northern

Mesopotamia. I'm referring of course to the geology, which is complex. Throughout our journey, we came across the three basic types of rock at various points:

Sedimentary – such rocks come about when small particles are laid down in water or when minerals in other rocks are acted upon by rain, snow or ice. Examples of sedimentary rocks are: limestone, sandstone and shale. They are commonly layered, and fossils are often preserved in sedimentary rocks.

Igneous – these rocks originate in fiery conditions when lava or magma becomes solid after cooling. Examples of igneous rocks are: granite, obsidian, pumice, basalt, andesite and tuff.

Metamorphic – rocks of this kind come into existence through great heat and/or pressure and also reactive fluids being exerted on or coming into contact with pre-existing rocks. Examples of metamorphic rocks are: marble, slate, shist and quartzite.

In addition, there is the seismic makeup of this part of the world which continues to exert an influence on not only this area, but also all of Türkiye in general and even neighbouring countries. Seismic events do not respect political boundaries. While most of the country sits on what is called the Anatolian tectonic plate, three other plates – the Eurasian, African and Arabian – all impinge on the seismic structure of Northern Mesopotamia. As a result of the interaction between these tectonic plates, earthquakes and tremors do occur in the region, sometimes with frightening and lethal consequences.

Church of St Peter/St Pierre, Antakya

We arrived at a hillside setting with a commanding view of Antakya where we entered the Church of St Pierre. It is reputed to be the first Christian church instituted by the Apostle, St Peter, who went on to become the Patriarch of Antioch and first Pope in Rome. He was later martyred there under the Roman emperor, Nero. The church was built into the mountainside, which is largely made up of limestone rock.

Parts of the church date from the 4th century CE and remnants of mosaics and frescoes near the altar can be seen. Murad informed us that there is a plentiful water supply to the church, which the early Christians used for baptism and for drinking. Because of the constant threat of attack to the Christians in this area at the time, an extensive tunnel system in the hillside adjacent to St Peter's Church provided a means of escape and protection.

The church was extended during the era of the Crusades in the 11th century and is now a museum.

Pointing to the altar stone, Murad asked me, "Nicholas, do you know what the symbols are and what they represent?" Our tour guide was referring to the use of the letters, Alpha (A) and Omega (ω), the first and last letters of the Greek alphabet clearly etched into the front of the altar. I explained that from what I was taught, this signifies the completeness of God and, according to the Christian belief as written in the Book of Revelations in the Old Testament of the Bible, Jesus Christ, as God, proclaims he is the beginning (Alpha [α/A]) and the end (Omega [ω/Ω]); God also possesses the power of immortality and is eternal.

At this point, although I didn't mention it to Murad, an old spiritual rumbling of scepticism bubbled up from my past, but I remained shtum in case any offence might be caused. Let me now try to elaborate on these mental meanderings of mine.

First off, I'm not a theologian nor can I claim any qualifications in these spiritual matters, but while I can attempt to grasp the concept of the 'almightyness' of God's claim to eternity and immortality, I've always been troubled by the use of the Alpha and Omega in this context. Why?

Looked at from another viewpoint, this divine timeline could be construed to mean there is a finite start and finish to it, therefore conflicting with the godly claim to eternal existence: an existence without a beginning or an ending.

In addition, this way of thinking implies that time is linear, always progressing in a straight line and continually 'running out'. But modern thinking, based on a great deal of scientific research and philosophical exploration carried out over many years, has challenged this view. Now, time is considered to be a much more complicated subject defying easy explanation. Hey, what do I know?

With this complexity in mind, I am in agreement with the view expressed by St Augustine who wrote, "What is time then? If nobody asks me, I know; but if I were desirous to explain it to one that should ask me, plainly I do not know."

Vakıflı – an Armenian village

We drove to Vakıflı, an Armenian village of 100 people and apparently the only one of its kind still in existence in Türkiye, situated on the slopes of Musa Dağ, not far from Antakya. Vakıflı overlooks the Mediterranean Sea and is close to the frontier with Syria. We popped into the local church with a small museum attached to it displaying artefacts of Armenian culture. We noted that the village was very tranquil as we walked by orange groves and old stone houses. This is where we met up with four young local people and we chatted for a while. When they saw my camera, they asked if I could take their photo and there and then they struck a pose for me.

As we drove away from Vakıflı, our conversation turned to the troubled history existing for many years between Türkiye and Armenia, and a discussion took place about the tragic events of 1915 mired in controversy ever since. Whatever the truth is and while it was appreciated that this prickly subject with a bloody undertow was touched upon and not avoided, one was left with the realisation that more progress needs to be made in the 'truth and reconciliation department' before the Turkish and Armenian psyches can accept what really happened in the past between these two peoples. Shared histories, where there are tales of inhumanity spilling over into two groups of people who may live as neighbours but who may not have been very neighbourly to one another, remind me of my Irish roots. Since the 1600s, two warring tribes in the north of Ireland have been at each other's throats with suffering, bloodshed, apartheid and mutual hatred that never goes away being the unfortunate consequences of this lamentable co-existence.

It takes a superhuman effort to consign past enmity to where it belongs – the past.

The Moses Tree

In another part of the city on Defne Road, there is the iconic Antakyan landmark, the Moses Tree, reputedly more than 3,000 years old. It is said to have grown from the staff of Moses who, in company with the immortal man known to the Turkish people as Hızır, climbed to the top of a mountain and there Moses drank from a stream containing the water of life while his staff turned into a tree bearing leaves. This friend of Moses, Hızır, is reputed to be a legendary mystic figure who became a popular saint for sailors in distress.

The Titus Tunnel
(aka the Vespasianus Titus Tunnel)

After a 20-minute drive on the D-420 south-west of Antakya, we reached the coastal town of Samandağ with the historic Titus Tunnel[4] nearby. A little inland from the sea, we climbed a hilly area with a gently rising pathway winding its way through an oasis of greenery where many wild flowers were to be seen. I could hear the sound of running water from a nearby stream and was grateful for the natural shade provided by the trees along our route.

As we got closer to the Titus Tunnel, we passed a solitary arched Roman bridge spanning a dry riverbed beneath. Moments later, we paused to take in the dramatic entrance to the tunnel complex which rose far above us on either side of where we stood. We descended into a giant chamber, which is not a natural phenomenon but was dug out by Roman legionnaires, sailors and prisoners under the direction of three emperors, Titus, Vespasian and Antonius, nearly 2,000 years ago. The reason these tunnels were created was that the ancient city of Seleucia Pieria (meaning 'Seleucia by the sea'), once an important Roman port, was under constant threat from floodwater that washed down from the nearby mountains. As these waters carried sediments and mud when they descended, the harbour area was becoming silted up and therefore unusable. By dint of sweated hard labour, the Titus Tunnel came into existence, which involved manual digging into the mountainside to divert the floodwaters by means of canals, tunnels and dams.

Seleucia Pieria itself served a valuable role in the export of goods coming from the East and onwards to Rome. It was from this place that St Barnabas and St Paul sailed on their missionary journeys.

As we walked through the first part of the tunnel, separated from the second section by an area open to the heavens, our tour guide asked us to imagine Seleucia Pieria as a thriving, populous trading centre by the sea where the shoreline of today is very different to what it was two millennia ago. We came across a rock with a Latin inscription on it which proclaimed, "*Divus Vespasianus et Divus Titus FC* (*Faciendum Curavit*)", ("Divine Vespasianus and Divine Titus caused it to be made").

With the towering walls above our heads, we couldn't help but be amazed at this incredible feat of engineering which helped to resolve the constant existential threat of inundation by the sea on the one hand and then from inland floodwater on the other.

Our spell at the Titus Tunnel concluded, we returned to our hotel in Antakya and had sufficient time to rest for the evening's activities.

Antakya by night – where everything flows in abundance

Just before we went out for the evening, I dashed out to get some more pictures before nightfall and during this jaunt on the streets near to our hotel, I came across this Aladdin's cave of an emporium full of interesting things. The shopkeeper saw me and invited me in. It was a treasure trove of stuff, not least the many silken goods on display. The gentleman (whose name was Yilmaz) proudly showed me his weaving loom and the various types of material he used. He also very kindly gave me a demonstration of his weaving expertise and, at my request, graciously posed for a photograph. I purchased a silk scarf for Rashida which Yilmaz had just woven.

Later, suitably dickeyed up for the evening, we adjourned to a nearby restaurant recommended to us, the Sveyka Restaurant, within a 5-minute stroll from our hotel and it was well worth the effort. It's a former *caravanserai** and on arrival we saw the place was packed, but fortunately a spare table was secured for us. We remarked on the pleasant atmosphere and having picked our waiter's brain, we dined on some local dishes he had suggested, such as the vishne kebab (sour cherry meatballs), makrube (an Antakyan dish of aubergine and spices), gia in the Hatay style with grilled chicken thighs served on a bed of humous – all delectable and generous portions served. Recalling this memorable meal is actually making me hungry as I write these words. We also tasted a local dry red wine, which complemented our dinner very well. Service was A+.

With our tummies well fed and our thirsts quenched, you'd think us oldies would be ready to snuggle under our respective duvets after such a long day but, oh no, the night owl gene inside the four of us sprang into life and off we set in search of music Antakya-style.

The prevailing temperature was ideal and as we walked about the city, there was a definite buzz about the place. We came across several caravanserais, cafés and bars with music of all sorts to be heard – jazz, modern and Turkish. Continuing our pub crawl, we popped into a few places to enjoy some local music, and where we might have downed a drink or three while taking a moment or two to savour the pleasure of this moment. I even picked up on local Antakya music which was a harmonious blend of Arabic and Turkish.

*River Asi
As it flows through the city of Antakya, this waterway is known as the River Asi. When it leaves the city and flows through the countryside on its way to the Mediterranean Sea, it becomes the Orontes River. Çelebi makes reference to the twin-named trait of this same river in his *Seyahatname*.

*Cradle of Civilisation
Whilst writing, I asked myself the question: "Is it possible, depending on where you come from in the world, that you may look on alternative 'cradles of civilisation' other than the Mesopotamian example I've quoted?"

I discovered the concept of a 'cradle of civilisation'[5] can apply to other places also. China, India and Egypt, for instance, possess their own cradles of civilisation in the Yellow River Basin, the Indus Valley and the Nile Basin respectively, which served as the regions where highly developed societies emerged in ancient times.

The whole idea of a cradle of civilisation stems from how a geographical area endowed with rivers yielding a plentiful water supply, fertile soil, a climate favourable to human habitation and conducive social and political factors were vital elements contributing to the birth of complex civilisations thousands of years ago.

*Caravanserai
No, not the music album of the same name, *Caravanserai*, an LP released by Carlos Santana in 1972 which, would you believe, I owned a vinyl copy of as a teenager and when my father heard me listening to it once, referred to this music as "drivel". But I held to a different outlook: a hunger to explore things new, including music.

How can I ever forget that iconic dreamy-blue record sleeve cover with a desert camel train visible in the middle distance dwarfed by an oversized orange orb of a sun. And memorable tracks with fantasy-inducing titles such as 'Eternal Caravan of Reincarnation', 'Song of the Wind' and 'All the Love of the Universe' for some reason penetrated deep into the psyche of a 17-year-old version of me. But I've digressed.

Caravanserai is, in fact, a very old Persian word meaning 'caravan palace'. It refers to a roadside inn where travellers could rest and seek refreshment to recuperate from their day's journey as they made their way along the ancient Silk Road trade route which connected China to Europe via present-day India, Pakistan, Iran and Türkiye, with additional routes through what is now Iraq, Syria and Egypt. Caravanserais had a commercial function where ambassadors, merchants and any travellers could stay while their possessions or goods could be stored safely from the hazards of the highway and, if transporting livestock, the animals had a place where they too could be fed and watered. Caravanserais also served as places where information, news and ideas could be shared and passed on.

Caravanserais were used as a means of official quarantine to stop the spread of serious diseases or epidemics such as cholera, smallpox or the plague.

Many caravanserais in use today in Türkiye date from the Middle Ages but history informs us that these hostelries of antiquity date back even further. Darius I, ruler of the Achaemenid Empire of the 5th–6th centuries BCE, had a Royal Road constructed that was 2,500 km (1,600 miles) in length running from Sardis (capital of the ancient kingdom of Lydia, now called Sart in modern Türkiye) to Susa (part of the ancient Elamite and Seleucid empires, now called Shush in modern Iran) and at various intervals along this important highway of old, the Silk Road, the forerunner of caravanserais came into being.

Also called the Silk Route, the Silk Road was not a single highway but a network of roads along the 8,000 km (5,000 miles) distance it covered connecting China with Europe. Serving as an historic forerunner of globalisation, the Silk Road not only enabled long-distance trade and commerce to flourish in the past, but it also aided in the inter-continental transmission of ideas long before the advent of newspapers and other media familiar to us now.

Also, it should not be overlooked that there was a nautical component to the Silk Road, as there was the Maritime Silk Road which operated for about 1,500 years from the 2nd century BCE up to the Middle Ages, with ships laden with cargo sailing to and from China via south-east Asia, the Arabian Peninsula, North Africa and Europe.

And now, well into the 21st century, there is the New Silk Road – a foreign policy initiative undertaken by China which has already cost $1trillion. Watch this space.

Perhaps the story of the Silk Road from earliest times to the present demonstrates an enduring aspect to the inherent character of humanity: that people will exploit a resource to maximum advantage where a sliding scale of enlightened self-interest is a factor.

The Orhan family, who serve the most delicious tepsi kebab.

Tepsi kebab, an Antakyan speciality.

Künefe, a delicious cheese-filled pastry with syrup and pistachios.

Aleppo *noria* or water wheel on the Orontes River, Syria.

Asi Bridge over Orontes River, Antakya.

Entrance to St Pierre Church, set in a cave.

Altar of St Pierre Church, showing symbolism of the Alpha (A) and the Omega (ω).

Vakıflı, an Armenian village close to Antakya.

Four young people seen in the Armenian village of Vakıflı.

The Moses Tree, Antakya.

Titus Tunnel, Samandağ – note the immense scale of water engineering,
dating back to the 1st century CE.

The coastal resort of Samandağ, near the Titus Tunnel.

The Roman arch over dry riverbed near the entrance to the Titus Tunnel, Samandağ.

Spanish broom (yellow flower), Titus Tunnel, Samandağ.

Granado Pomegranate, Titus Tunnel, Samandağ.

Two local beauties, Feray and Rashida, posing at the Titus Caves.

Evening street scene, Antakya.

Street murals, including a depiction of the Asi Bridge and the Orontes River, Antakya.

Street market, Antakya.

The shop of Mr Yilmaz, where I learnt about silk weaving, Antakya.

Mr Yilmaz seen weaving on his silken loom, Antakya.

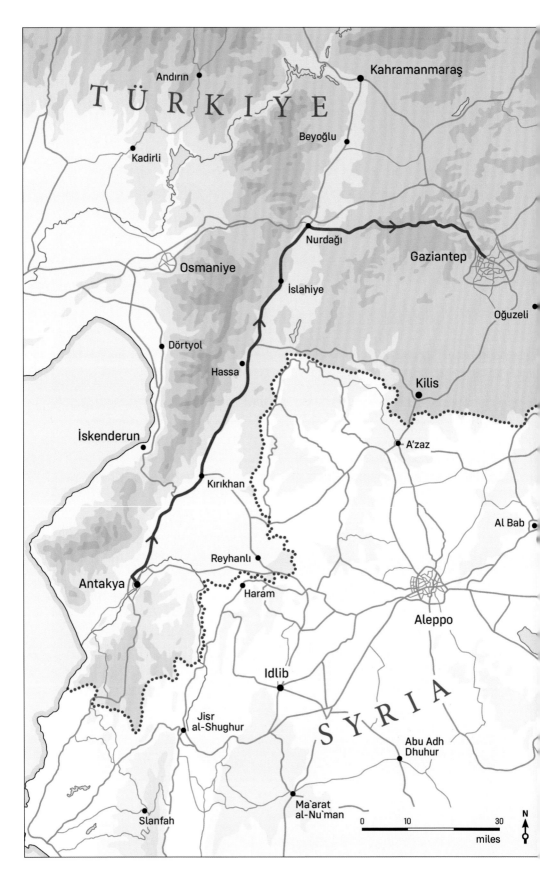

SATURDAY 25TH MAY 2019

Amazing breakfast – Antakya-style
and onwards through antiquity

let our thoughts
connect
freely
to uncover
the way and the truth

PROPOSED ITINERARY:
▷ Hatay Archaeological Museum, Antakya
▷ Depart Antakya and drive to Gaziantep
▷ Check into Gaziantep hotel
▷ Explore Gaziantep, local museum, castle and market
▷ Tahmis Kahvesi, renowned 17th-century coffee house
▷ Enjoy dinner of local cuisine and afterwards music at Millethan

The following morning we had an early start and were served a magnificent breakfast with a definitive Antakyan 'accent' where paprika, for example, was used plentifully to complement some cream cheese, an omelette and humous, which was also served with local olives, tomatoes, cucumber and big bunches of parsley.

Murad joined as we finished off our early morning spread and by 9.45am we were on the road again, heading straight for the second largest mosaic museum in the world: the Hatay Archaeological Museum.

As soon as we entered the museum, we were struck by the huge scale of the interior space given over to the striking display of a vast number of mosaics. It was a feast of mammoth proportions for the senses. We gazed in wonder at classical Greek and Roman scenes depicting the mythological figures of Dionysus, Orpheus, Diana and Venus, as well as many other characters from the sagas of the ancients.

Also on display were the interiors of what must have been from well-to-do households dating back 2,000 years which possessed stunning artistic representations of human figures, hunting scenes, wildlife and geometric patterns. Imagine what it must have been like living in such classical grandeur when at home in these ancient times. But many of these classical interiors were excavated under pressure from where they had lain undisturbed in the Hatay province for nearly two millennia. Archaeologists often had to work quickly to recover these irreplaceable relics of the past as modern life now intervened. Why this time constraint? Fast forward to today: over the past 30 years, the Turkish government has been in the process of upgrading the local infrastructure and this included large-scale engineering works designed to enhance the water supply to the region. The planned construction of reservoirs, canals and dams although benefitting the population of the area was, however, putting at risk and, in some cases, threatening the destruction of these ancient artefacts including many unique mosaics – discovered at varying intervals over the last century.

With the clock ticking, contemporary archaeologists therefore worked at pace to excavate these valuables of long ago and the Hatay Museum served as the new resting place of this rescued treasure. This proved to be a complex and challenging task as these mosaics would have been photographed *in situ* to record accurately their appearance. With each bit of the mosaic carefully numbered and logged, the painstaking methodology of dismantling and removal piece by piece would have followed. Transportation to the Hatay Museum was the next step and the final act of this remarkable process of recreating the past occurred when the mosaics were reassembled, again piece by piece, and restored to their original magnificence for the world to marvel at.

Sacrificial altars, columns, statues and frescoes dating back to the Hattian or Hittite period of 2,000 years BCE up to the Roman period were also unearthed and placed in the museum. It has been a remarkable achievement, as the curators have striven hard to reconstruct a true depiction of these antiquities within their original ancient setting. This Hatay Museum was established in 1934 and it has handsomely added to its collection of mosaics over the intervening years.

We came to understand how this extraordinary place is the embodiment of what the founding father of modern Türkiye, Mustafa Kemal Atatürk, had prescribed for a forward-looking nation: "The Republic of Türkiye is built on culture," while recognising that it is vital to safeguard the past in order to carve out a meaningful future.

Murad helpfully started out by giving us an overview of the timelines that were used not only by the Hatay Archaeological Museum, but also in other museums and historical sites we'd be stopping at over the coming days.

As we continued our tour of the museum, Murad told us about the many artefacts on show. When we stopped to look at the Star of David mosaic, our tour guide explained how this was an object of fascination as this innovative design has resonance in many cultures in many locations around the world and stretching over vast time spans.[6]

Archaeological artefacts that have the Star of David on them can be divided into types according to:

▷ the place where they were discovered, such as a synagogue, a church or a monastery, a mosque;

▷ the language inscribed around them, such as Hebrew, Latin, Greek, Arabic, Sanskrit;

▷ adjacent symbols such as a Menorah, a Cross, a Crescent.

To give you an inkling into the complexity, variety and sense of importance attached to the Star of David, the following list is arranged in chronological order starting with the earliest known existence of this striking imagery:

A. Stars of David used for commercial purposes or for decoration.
B. Pagan Stars of David.
C. Jewish Star of David.
D. Christian Star of David.
E. Muslim Star of David.
F. Indian Star of David.

In addition to these, the following Stars of David were also found:

G. Assyrian Stars of David.
H. Stars of David in the Mayan culture of southern America.

Researchers generally indicate the non-Jewish Star of David by the name Hexagram. Hexagram is a name invented only relatively recently; it was not known for thousands of years how the non-Jewish Stars of David were named. 'Hex' is the Greek word that represents the number six, 'gram' means line. Even the Christian name for the Shield of David, 'the Star of David' only appeared in recent centuries. Muslims called the Star of David the Seal of Solomon, but the Seal of Solomon was used both in Judaism and in Islam, also as the name of a pentagram. The Indian Star of David is commonly named Yantra.

Murad told us that many of the mosaics on show had been rescued from private houses of the classical period, later inundated because of the construction of river dams for water management and irrigation purposes. He went on to say that he believed that the museum only shows a fraction of the many mosaics and other archaeological artefacts that have now been lost due to the dam-building programme.

This prompted a discussion among the five of us about the competing needs of the past versus the present: the contemporary requirements of the local region to have an adequate water supply were met with the building of reservoirs. A careful balancing act has been maintained: the link to the past has been preserved with the artefacts being moved from their historical site to the Hatay Museum; the past is not lost.

At this point, Murad first aired his theory of cultural development and asked what the main 'driver' is for civilisation and social evolution? This was most definitely a 'big question' which our tour guide, we came to learn, was in the habit of posing on a regular basis, not simply to test the charges under his care, i.e. us, the quartet, but also, we felt, to test himself, to the core of his inner beliefs and perhaps ours also. What drives social evolution? We were scratching our heads to come up with a decent response and while doing so, I was of the view that Murad's query would have kept a school of learned scholars busy for yonks.

Murad, tongue in cheek, responded with this: 'The Theory of Advancing Civilisation' that as far as he was concerned, was women who were the driving force for social evolution. In his own family, Murad described himself as the breadwinner and his wife as the homemaker. Similarly, he believed that in the past, women were responsible for social changes. In his view, when one family in antiquity possessed a beautiful mosaic, the wife of the next-door neighbour would have desired something even more beautiful. And so on and so forth on a variation on a theme of one-upmanship, ahem, one-upwomanship or…

But seriously, this question of social change touches on many complex and fundamental issues which go way beyond the scope of the chat we were having with our tour guide.

After passing through the museum shop, we took our leave of Antakya at a little after 1pm and as we drove on, I reflected on our stay in this remarkable setting on the eastern Mediterranean.

I must admit I was in complete agreement with the Ottoman explorer Evliya Çelebi, who had frequented this spot some 360 years previously, as I had come to appreciate that Antakya is still a beautiful city and one of the most delightful places in the world. Further references to Evliya Çelebi are to be seen on Days 1, 5 and 8.

We now set off on a two-and-a-half hour road trip to Gaziantep, covering 196 km (122 miles). Murad selected a northern route along the D-825 and then struck a path eastwards at a place called Nurdaği and we followed the D-400 all the way until we reached our destination.

For those transportation nerds among you, please note the D-400 is a state highway in southern Türkiye, 2,057 km (1,278 miles) in length, with an east–west orientation starting at Datça in the south-west corner of the Anatolian peninsula and ending at the Iranian border at Esendere.

As our MPV trundled along those well-paved Turkish highways in the early afternoon sunshine, we chatted a little. Later, Feray, Suat and Rashida nodded off, with even Murad getting some shut-eye. Our driver, Halil and I remained awake.

Halil, who was calm-natured, kept his eyes on the road and I was relaxed with his style of driving, safe but swift and very much in control. He never spoke when behind the steering wheel. I gazed at the passing parade of the vastness of the Turkish landscape: mountains, valleys, villages, rivers, fields, bridges and the infrequent vehicle rolled by.

I took advantage of this quiet moment to scribble an update in my notebook and, at some point, I must have paused in my scribblings to look out of the window. My eyes came to rest on a mountain with contours and colours which took me back to my student days in Ireland. Back to the autumn of 1973, and I had followed in my father's footsteps and was an undergraduate at Trinity College, but instead of choosing history as my main subject of interest (as my father had done in the 1940s), I opted for the natural sciences. This entailed a study of chemistry, mathematics, statistics, psychology, biology, economics, geology and geography. And why natural sciences? Rebellion, I guess, as my father wanted me to read history at Trinity as I had become steeped in the humanities, classics and languages during my school career. But I was 17 and contrary, so a compromise was reached: I would go to TCD but my choice of subject prevailed. When I look back on it now across an arc of half a century, I'm so glad I stuck to my guns as I learnt so much from my exploration of the scientific world. This experience helped to rebalance my understanding of two academic spheres often at loggerheads with each other: the arts and the sciences. But I have always borne in mind my father's sage advice regarding the pursuit of history: *Procedere sine praeiudicio* (Proceed without bias).

Back to the present, as this Turkish outcrop of rock bore an uncanny resemblance to a long-extinct volcano in south County Dublin called the Sugarloaf Mountain. Suddenly, my mind swarmed with ideas and memories which I felt worth documenting, not forgetting what I'd originally started doing – recording our stay in this part of Northern Mesopotamia.

No doubt prompted by our philosophical discussions earlier on, the influence of the Turkish scenery sparking a series of flashbacks, an amalgam of ideas and memories floated into my consciousness and vied for my attention as we sped on to Gaziantep. Being of 'a certain age' with the ever-present spectre of senior moments getting in the way of clear thinking and all that tomfoolery, I began to jot down furiously my thoughts lest I forgot.

The first of these sparkings from overactive synaptic gaps I'll call Geological Spirituality. Perhaps, this is one of the great benefits of travel: it offers us the chance to think in ways where boundaries melt away and new, exciting vistas swim into view. OK, so let's delve into Geological Spirituality.

Let me take you back to October 1973. It's late afternoon on what had been a crisp, dry and sunny Saturday and along with my fellow first-year science students of Trinity College Dublin, we're milling about in the fading autumn light on the platform of

Killiney railway station awaiting the return train to Dublin. It's been a cracking day. We've just completed our first geological field trip to look at the sedimentary and igneous rock formations, the granites, minerals and fossils in south County Dublin bordering Wicklow. We've also learnt about the ancient volcano (now extinct) that is iconic to all Dubliners, known as the Sugarloaf Mountain. Our group of fledgling geologists was being looked after by a personable and erudite lecturer, Dr S – himself not long graduated from Cambridge – who had been enthusing our eager minds and I can remember feeling a great sense of excitement at the prospect of learning about this fascinating subject. But I was also a little scared as there was so much new 'stuff' to take in. In particular, I was taken aback by the huge stretches of time that geology appeared to deal in as a normality bordering on insouciance that I felt was way beyond human comprehension. As an 18-year-old undergraduate, I could get my head around years, decades or centuries or, at a stretch, a millennium. But anything more was beyond me.

There was something else though which was causing something of a mental conflict at that moment half a century ago. My mongrel religious education (largely Anglican and Presbyterian, not forgetting the Catholic influence from my mother) thanks to my father's King James Bible had categorically stated in the Book of Genesis of the Old Testament that God had formed the earth in 4,004 BCE, i.e. 5,977 years previously – don't forget I'm referring to 1973, some 50 years previous to this historical excursion to south-east Türkiye.

But in stark contrast to the religious foundational way of thinking about the formation of the earth and all that went with it, these geological experts counted their eras in millions and billions of years and I felt my mind reeling as I wondered about so many things at this point: how did they know that something was a million or a billion years old; why were the geologists so blasé about all this; how come these geologists could teach these details (erroneous perhaps from a religious viewpoint) about the formation of the earth that flew in the face of what I'd learnt as a youngster from my Bible classes and, most puzzling of all, what exactly is a million or a billion years?

With all this jumbled up, historical stuff intertwined with newly learned scientific information flitting about in my brain, I approached Dr S as we stood on the suburban station platform and attempted to pose my anguished questions seeking comprehension. How was I to learn to inhabit this mightily expanded and unfamiliar expanse of time that appeared to undermine a core spiritual belief about the formation of our planet even if I could not count myself as a practising Christian at the age of 18?

In the minutes before the arrival of the train, Dr S gently put my overwrought mind at rest in a manner I'll never forget as he encouraged me to free my thinking from a theological mindset. The academic went further and inspired me to make good use of my imagination in the pursuit of the study of geology. "Just let your imagination flow freely," was his guiding phrase which I've never forgotten.

Secondly, concerning the geological eras and how to commit to memory, he taught me the following mnemonic, '**C**amels **O**ften **S**it **D**own **C**arefully **P**erhaps **T**heir **J**oints **C**reak' – this nonsensical ditty has helped me to remember all the lengthy epochs as **C**ambrian, **O**rdovician, **S**ilurian, **D**evonian, **C**arboniferous, **P**ermian, **T**riassic, **J**urassic and **C**retaceous. Subsequent eras running up to the present were covered by a particular favourite of mine: **P**igeon **E**gg **O**melettes **M**ake **P**eople **P**uke **R**egularly which acted as a reminder for **P**alaeocene, **E**ocene, **O**ligocene, **M**iocene, **P**liocene, **P**leistocene and **R**ecent; the Recent era being the geological period we are living in now. Dr S went on to point out that the Cambrian dates back some 600 million years and since geologists believe that the 'Big Bang' theory of the formation of our universe occurred some 5–6 billion years ago, the young academic drew our attention to the fact that the Pre-Cambrian era was the longest epoch of all, stretching back more than 4 billion years to the distant dawn of the cosmos as we know it.

I remember vividly that flash of awareness, inspiration or whatever you might call it when my brain understood I was capable of entertaining more than one 'big idea' in my mind at the same time. A door somewhere had sprung open, enabling me to feel at ease when considering differing views on the same subject. I was free to evaluate the various merits of the concepts under analysis and, after weighing up the arguments and counter arguments, come to my own conclusion. A statement of the bleedin' obvious, you might say, and I'd be the first to agree, but for me at that age it was a turning point when I realised it was possible to perform this simple yet profound mental exercise at any time, in any way I wished at a time of my choosing.

It was with a sense of immense relief, therefore, that I stepped onto the Dublin-bound train on that long-past autumn day. A pivotal moment had occurred in how I viewed the passage of time and freedom of thought. There's been no looking back since.

In a way, this enlightened approach chimed with the teachings of a maverick Jesuit priest I had had the good fortune to meet in the early 1970s who challenged me in my beliefs and went on to tell me that if I were to treat all other human beings without causing harm in the way I'd like to be treated myself, then not only would I be fulfilling Christian values but also the tenets of the world's major religions. It was another one of those eye-opener moments in my young life. One thing this Jesuit minister told me in response to my query about the obligations imposed on Christians to believe in God resonates to this day as he batted back at me: "You are under no obligation to believe in God."

My sister and I had a very liberal upbringing where our parents placed great emphasis on learning and instilling in us the freedom to think for ourselves. When

I think back on this now, the geologist, the priest and my parents were all aligned in their delivery of a similar message.

By the way, please note I will touch on further mental meanderings when opportune moments present themselves later on in the book. You have been warned.

Back to the present and our tour of Northern Mesopotamia embraced by the Euphrates and the Tigris rivers, where our tour guide had expounded earlier on humanitarian beliefs but on this occasion from an Islamic perspective where, as a practising Muslim, he treated all other human beings as he wished to be treated himself. At this point, I recalled the idea of a continuous thread of profound meaning – where goodness is an essential element – that connects the beginning of one's life with its later years, and I marvelled at how an Irish priest and a Turkish tour guide separated by more than 50 years had in a way helped to complete this special link in such an amazing and personal way. Experience shows us there's a knack to spotting 'goodness' in people no matter where they come from, their religion or social standing. Countless thinkers, philosophers and theologians have written on the subject of being good or leading a moral life but if I had to choose one figure from this long list, I would select Plato, who studied under Socrates and who, in turn, was a tutor to Aristotle.

In his magnum opus *Republic* (it's a rough translation of the original Greek title, Πολιτεία [Politeea] which can also mean 'state' or 'political system'). At its heart, Plato's *Republic* is an in-depth examination of the moral life and how to lead one, thus hopefully leading to harmony in society. This seminal work, including a series of dialogues, meanders through a richly textured metaphysical landscape which seeks to offer insight into how one should live one's life. It is said that Plato mapped out the general schemata for philosophy more than 2,300 years ago and philosophers have been filling in the gaps ever since.

It is interesting to note that Plato's writings and those of other classical Greek scholars were translated into Arabic by the Iraqi polymath, Abu Yusuf Al-Kindi who lived in the 9th century CE. Al-Kindi is considered to be a leading figure in the field of Arabic philosophy.

This subject of the cross-fertilisation of ideas is further touched upon subsequently on Day 5 when I talk about the life and times of Thabit al-Harrani.

This cascade of thoughts, ideas, memories, dreams and mental meanderings carried on uninterrupted until we reached the outskirts of our next stop, Gaziantep. I remember asking of myself if I had truly adhered to this simple but profound axiom of being a good human being during my earthly existence; a touchstone of morality which transcends all beliefs in any age.

At this point, Rashida, Feray, Suat and Murad stirred from their respective slumbers as our MPV slowed to a crawl through dense traffic.

Gaziantep – with an extraordinary
history and an enchanting ambience

First things first: on arrival, Murad granted Feray her wish and took us to a charming tree-lined square in the centre of Gaziantep as we were hot on the trail of seeking out the best künefe – a local sweet dish made from mozzarella white cheese, honey and pistachios. Feray's craving for something sweet was satisfied beyond measure.

I'm glad to report that Murad's excellent nose for such tasty commodities proved to be spot on as we descended on the Činaraltı establishment and watched the experts do their magic in front of us. The künefe was superb.

Afterwards, we went to check into our hotel, the Hişvahan, an old inn (Turkish: *han*) fully restored only three years previously in 2016. As new arrivals, we'd been told by the staff that the walls of the hotel dated back nearly 450 years to 1577 and we learnt our *han* was one of the many caravanserais which had formed part of a vast network of trade routes criss-crossing Asia, north Africa and south-eastern Europe, the most notable being the old Silk Road.

As it was mid-afternoon in Ramadan, the hotel courtyard was very quiet and the restaurant was empty. We were shown our rooms which were spacious, comfortable and on a grand scale but with a weird difference. When staying in Turkish hotels of all shapes and sizes, one had become used to accommodation where natural light streamed in through windows. But this *han* was unlike anything experienced previously and had an unusual modern twist to the interior décor. Our room was illuminated with recessed artificial lighting and black window curtains were hanging from the ceiling to the floor. Further black drapes surrounded the bed and this boudoir-style design had an additional red accent in its soft furnishings.

After freshening up, we were out on the road again as Murad led the way, walking towards our next port of call: Gaziantep Castle, which overlooked our hotel from a nearby hill.

We learnt that this castle dates back 2,000 years, having first been constructed by the Romans who occupied the area when it was on the eastern fringes of their empire. This hilltop fortress was added to by different peoples who had conquered the region over the years and we entered this enormous edifice to view the military museum inside. It proved to be dark and on the austere side with none of the explanations for the exhibits translated into English as we'd experienced before in Turkish museums. The abiding impression I was left with was that it was a very serious show of military history with overbearing displays; some of which were life-sized metallic sculptures of former members of the Turkish armed forces and political figures.

We climbed up to the ramparts of the castle which gave us a commanding 360 degree panorama of Gaziantep and the surrounding area. At this point, thanks to Murad's explanations, it was made clear why this vantage point on high was of such value to any military force which controlled the area. One could see for miles and thus the approach of an enemy from any direction could be detected easily, giving the defenders ample time for suitable counter measures to be taken to deal with an invader.

While on the ramparts of Gaziantep Castle, Murad and Suat talked about the Hittites, their origins and how ancient warfare changed with the invention of new weaponry and tactics, the more effective use of infantry and artillery thus enabling a small military force to overcome a larger army using an obsolete method of warfare. It was also noted that when one conqueror took over, there wasn't a clean break between one culture/people replacing the (weaker) predecessor, it was more a case of overlap between the conquered and conqueror, so mixing and integration took place.

And since we're discussing the Hittites, I did some research into their numeral system, such as the numbers one to ten and the vocabulary of basic words like water, father, mother or eat. Also, this reminded me of an intriguing encounter I had in Jeddah, Saudi Arabia many years ago with a former major in the Pakistani army. He knew I was from Ireland and he asked me to count one to ten in Irish which I duly did: 1-aon, 2-dó, 3-trí, 4-ceathair, 5-cúig, 6-sé, 7-seacht, 8-acht, 9-naoi, 10-deich. He expressed surprise as he told me that some of these words sounded very similar to his native tongue, Urdu[7] and its classical antecedent, Sanskrit[8] dating back 3,500 years.

As I've always been very interested in languages, and since we've been dwelling on the subject a wee while, I thought I'd draw up a small linguistic comparison chart with a (near) global perspective, opposite.

Gaziantep was previously called Antep, but from the 1920s, after the French occupation when 7,000 local people were reportedly killed, the city was renamed Gaziantep. The Turkish government took this step to honour its citizens and soldiers who valiantly put up a struggle against the invading forces. The Turkish word *gazi* means veteran. This bloody episode took place during a little-known period of strife known as the Franco-Turkish War which lasted from 1918-1921, following the secret Sykes-Picot Agreement signed in 1916 between the British and the French designed to carve up portions of the Ottoman Empire to be taken over and administered by these two allied powers in conflict with Türkiye. It is interesting to note that a large contingent of Armenian soldiers fought under the French flag and were based in the region during this brief period.

The weather so far during our time in Northern Mesopotamia had been amazing, as it was sunny and dry with day temperatures ranging from the mid to high 20s Celsius.

English	Irish	Sanskrit	Urdu	Hittite	Latin	Turkish	Chinese
one	aon	eka	aik	siya	unus	bir	yi
two	dó	dvi	dow	dau	duo	iki	er
three	trí	tri	teen	teri	tres	üç	san
four	ceathair	catur	chaar	meyu	quattuor	dört	si
five	cúig	panca	paanch	-	quinque	beş	wu
six	sé	sat	chay	-	sex	altı	liu
seven	seacht	sapta	saat	siptam	septem	yedi	qi
eight	acht	asta	aath	-	octo	sekiz	ba
nine	naoi	nava	now	-	novem	dokuz	jiu
ten	deich	dasa	das	-	decem	on	shi
water	uisce	ap	ab	waatar	aqua	su	shui
eat	ithe	atti	chabana	ezzateni	edere	yemek	chi
bread	arán	pupah	roti	harsi	panis	ekmek	mianbao
mother	máthair	matr	ma	anna	mater	anne	mama
father	athair	tata	pidar	attas	pater	baba	baba
to me	domsa	-	-	mi	ad me	bana	duì wǒ lái shuō
to you	chugat	-	-	ti	tibi	size	gei ni

Note the amazing similarities in some of these words despite the diversity of language families, the geographical distances involved and the enormous time period or era differences separating them and yet the word for 'three' or 'seven' enjoys a widespread similarity, except for Turkish and Chinese.

I was also fascinated to see that the Hittite words dating back 3-4,000 years for 'water' and 'to me' are so like their contemporary English equivalents.[9] The Irish word for father, '*athair*', is not too dissimilar from its Hittite equivalent, '*attas*'. Intriguing to observe the Hittite and Turkish for mother are virtually identical.

My Pakistani friend (quoted opposite) was spot on about the numbers in Irish and Sanskrit resembling each other.

Sanskrit, Urdu, Chinese and Hittite words have been transliterated into English (romanised) script.

When we left the castle, Murad took us on a walking tour. After an easy stroll of ten minutes, we arrived at the large market which was a well laid-out, covered structure in the centre of town. I noted the predominance of Turkish flags about the place. There were many shops selling all manner of wares and we came across a silk seller who bade us enter his place of business. Turned out that the two men running the place, who spoke good English, were from just down the road so to speak, 75 miles away in Aleppo in neighbouring war-torn Syria with family still there.

One of the men told me how he had gone back to Aleppo the previous year, knowing it was dangerous but he wanted to see his family. On his return journey his luck ran out when he was apprehended by armed men and put in prison. He was only released on payment of a 'fine'. This man said that several million Syrians like him are refugees in Türkiye and he's very grateful that the Turkish government have let them stay. He now runs a shop in Gaziantep with a business partner (whom we also met) selling silk merchandise. The positive demeanour of this man impressed me and he spoke openly about his recent experiences. I observed he talked without rancour against the Syrian regime – all he wanted was for peace and normality to return. I was moved by this man's humanity and wished him well as we parted.

As I left the market, I reflected on how this Syrian refugee had been forced out of his native land due to a protracted and bloody civil war where countless others have suffered. It is sad beyond belief. It is estimated that over 500,000 people have perished, with those injured and displaced numbering in the millions. Officially, 3.5 million Syrian refugees are being accommodated in Türkiye, and the Turkish government deserves credit for their humanitarian intervention in providing shelter to so many people uprooted by this Armageddon of a struggle. No other country in the world has been as welcoming to these victims of a war that continues to rage in a neighbouring land whose border is not that far off from various places we visited during our trip. Anecdotally, however, it is thought that more than 5 million Syrians have found their way into Türkiye, many unofficially. Whatever the true number of Arabic-speaking immigrants of all ages and from all walks of life who have ended up in Türkiye, the quartet discussed how incredibly complex this situation is. One serious challenge facing this host nation is one of integration.

We came to learn the serving Gaziantep mayor, Fatma Şahin, has adopted a number of measures to assimilate the 500,000+ Syrian people – yes, you read that correctly: Gaziantep, previously 1.5 million souls, has provided a refuge to half a million Syrians and so increasing the population of the city by a third.

As an aside, it should be noted that many refugees and economic migrants not only from Syria but elsewhere have used Türkiye as a corridor to reach mainland Europe to seek a new life.

Mayor Fatma Şahin, in office since 2014, was mentioned in the *Daily Sabah*, a Turkish newspaper, which talked about the development of "… municipal projects for the economic and social inclusion of Syrian refugees…" (*Daily Sabah* Economy Editor, Elif Binici, in conversation with Gaziantep Mayor Fatma Şahin; March 2018).

In creating the model for 'co-habitation' with Syrians and Turks living side by side, Mayor Şahin initiated a number of programmes which were focused on key issues such as housing, education, health, jobs, municipal services and the challenging area of social cohesion. The mayor stated:

> *We have developed a Gaziantep model … in which our children go to school with Syrian refugee children. We have included refugee women and children in all the social aid programmes that we have organised … (which) … include teaching them Turkish and providing psychosocial counselling services.*
>
> *Daily Sabah* Economy Editor, Elif Binici, in conversation with Gaziantep Mayor Fatma Şahin, March 2018

It would appear that when faced with the challenge of accommodating a large influx of Syrian refugees to the city, Gaziantep Mayor Şahin and her administration adopted a pragmatic approach underpinned with a sense of humanity.

With the persistent plight of Syrian refugees in mind, more recently in May 2021, it was reported that Nikolaus Meyer-Landrut, the head of an EU delegation to Türkiye, was visiting Sanliurfa (Urfa) where he was looking into how a city deals with the challenges posed by a large influx of refugees.[10] Mr Meyer-Landrut noted that the authorities of Sanliurfa are working on finding solutions to the situation where EU support has been forthcoming with a focus on vocational training, and both he and his team availed of the opportunity to see Göbeklitepe, described as the cradle of humanity where the world's oldest temple is located and which has also been listed as a UNESCO world heritage site – please see relevant section, Day 5.

Most recent evidence suggests, however, that the attitude towards the Syrian refugees may have changed in Türkiye, with confrontations and even violence reported between local people and the new arrivals.

> *seen from distant space,*
> *earthly borders*
> *are invisible,*
> *meaningless.*
> *So, why not in our minds?*

I'm well aware I've touched on a sensitive subject where countries have a right to protect their interests when they feel they might be under some pressure, or even threat, when permitting foreigners to enter their territory to stay temporarily or to put down roots and settle, becoming citizens in this 'new' country. It is a question fraught with problems and complexity, I grant you, but, if I may suggest, it does need to be approached in a positive way, enabling all the interested parties to work collaboratively on this whole issue guided by compassion.

After all, as an Irishman I've formed part of the large Irish diaspora and was made welcome in Britain where I now live with my family. But it wasn't so long ago when immigrants were confronted with rude notices when seeking a roof over their heads from English landlords such as, "Accommodation available. No dogs, no blacks, no Irish", being a common form of advertisement. Fortunately, society has moved on and this kind of racism is no longer acceptable, while also being against the law. Over the years, Irish people have found new homes and livelihoods in not only the UK but also in many countries around the world, with some making a name for themselves in their new lives away from the homeland.

One is the impressively named Ambrosio O'Higgins, an Irishman (originally from County Sligo) who had ventured to South America in the 18th century and who later became governor of Chile; his son, Bernardo O'Higgins (as I was told by my father when I was a teenager) went on to become a general in the Chilean army and is considered to be a founding father of Chile when it became free from Spanish rule.

Then there was Thomas Francis Meagher who took part in the Young Ireland Rebellion of 1848, but this Irish revolution against British rule was a failure and Meagher along with his fellow rebels were sentenced to death, later commuted to long terms of imprisonment in Australia. But Meagher managed to escape and made it to the United States, where, long story short, he went on to become a general in the Union Army during the American Civil War of 1861–65.

More recently, in the 20th century, the American artist Georgia O'Keefe, who was a leading exponent of abstract art, born in Michigan in 1887, had Irish ancestry, and the Hollywood star Maureen O'Hara, who appeared in many blockbuster films, was born and brought up in Dublin.

Could Ireland, reflecting on its history cognisant of the fact that so many people of Irish ancestry sought and gained a livelihood over the centuries in other lands across the globe, now possibly reconsider its role to make foreigners not only welcome on its shores but also able to be fully integrated into becoming Irish citizens of the future?

Our guide, Murad, informed us we couldn't come to Gaziantep without tasting another local delicacy: katmer. I noted the glint in his eye as he described this sweet titbit that used very fine filo pastry as a base mixed with a widely grown local nut, the pistachio, a member of the cashew family where the seeds of the pistachio tree are treated as food. Additional katmer ingredients are butter, sugar and clotted cream with ice cream a whimsical extra. We arrived at the shop-cum-café where we were greeted by members of the same family running this establishment called Metanet Katmer Salonu (Metanet Katmer Shop). Four brothers, the sons of the owner, proudly displayed the pastry they were selling and then invited us in to sit down in their café alongside the shop to taste their wares. We were aware that it was Ramadan and Murad had let us know that he was fasting, but he still sat with us as we enjoyed the local version of simit – a Turkish bagel smothered in sesame seeds and followed, of course, with lashings of katmer. As we tucked in, Murad told us how Gaziantep was a UNESCO-recognised gastronomic centre and enjoys a reputation for its quality of cuisine all over Türkiye. He went on to say that this city also possesses a mix of various cultures and cuisines within this portion of south-eastern Anatolia where pistachios are commonly grown.

Our katmer proved to be delightful and Murad then let us in on a Turkish marital secret: according to tradition, katmer is the first meal eaten by newly married couples in the morning after their first night together, as it represents the sweetness they hope to experience in their wedded bliss together.

Fed and watered, we went on a second walking tour and in the course of our wanderings we came across a beautifully fashioned type of door knocker that was in the shape of a miniature hand – this was to be seen on many front doors. Each of these sculpted hands possessed an artistic flourish and a charm all of its own. We naturally inquired and Murad first of all complimented us on our observation skills and then proceeded to enlighten us about the local practice of the three-way etiquette of using this nifty door knocker, so that depending on how it was used, it would alert the resident as to whether a lady, a gentleman or a child was calling.

By this stage, we were in need of sustenance again, naturally, so Murad rewarded our doughty exploration skills with a pit stop at the oldest coffee house in Gaziantep, known as the Tahmis Kahvesi, established in 1635. We enjoyed a flavourful pick-me-up in the form of freshly made Turkish coffee served in metal-covered cups, with mixed nuts as a snack. I think we all noted quietly to ourselves that here was Murad fasting from dawn to dusk – some 15 hours or so – in line with Islamic tradition during Ramadan and yet here we were as four visitors to Türkiye just about able to keep up with our full-of-beans tour guide but only if we replenished our energy reserves every few hours or so. How was he able to keep going? I admired Murad for this and also when he spoke enthusiastically about various areas of historical interest and what we might see on our trip, including a mountain to ascend, Mount Nemrut, with its famous unique statues of large carved stone heads at the summit, not to be confused with its lesser-known namesake on the western shore of Lake Van. Nemrut, Murad informed us, was a biblical character, great-grandson of Noah.

It was getting on for dusk. We passed a big square and we noticed lots of food being prepared with many tables and chairs being set up as if for a major communal event. This was *ifhtar*, the meal that breaks the daylong fast during Ramadan and the whole community was invited, thanks to the generosity of the local municipality. Crowds were gathering nearby and we encouraged Murad to go and break his fast. He promised to do so but before going he kindly assisted us with the booking of dinner at a local *han* called Bayazhan (meaning White House) with a solid reputation for good cuisine.

The night was still young and finding additional reserves of energy from who knows where after dinner, the quartet headed out for a stroll. No doubt about it but Gaziantep was abuzz. Many people of all ages were milling about and illuminated street decorations were plentiful.

We came across another ancient caravanserai that specialised in what we were searching for, Millethan (meaning Folk Inn), dating from 1562. There, we were treated to a medley of traditional music and song, and while we might have drunk a wee dram or two of the local hard stuff, I noted that Millethan was replete with statues of illustrious literary and historical figures going back a millennium. Of those sculpted likenesses on display, I noted Ibn Haldun (Khaldun), 1332–1406 CE who was a philosopher, historian and economist who lived and worked in north Africa. In his lifetime, he published a multi-volume 'universal history'.

Also on show was the bust of Imam-I Gazzali, 1058–1111 CE, a polymath who was born in the Seljuk Empire in what is now present-day Iran. His best-known work is a philosophical treatise with a hint of the oxymoron entitled *The Incoherence of the Philosophers*.

We trooped back to our hotel, the magnificent Hişvahan, and had to knock at the main gate, now closed, to gain entrance through a much smaller door – the night entrance. It had been an enthralling day in Gaziantep and we fell into our beds exhausted.

Breakfast, Antakya-style.

Entrance to the Hatay Archaeological Museum, Antakya, with a replica of a *noria* (water wheel).

Mosaic of Oceanus, Greek deity, son of Uranus, Hatay Archaeological Museum.

Greco-Roman mosaic from the 5th century CE, depicting cωτηρια (Sotiria), the Greek goddess of salvation, Hatay Archaeological Mueum.

Mosaic, abstract design, probably Roman, Hatay Archaeological Museum.

Birth of Venus mosaic, Hatay Archaeological Museum.

Primordial gods; Bronze Age, 3,300-1,200 BCE, Hatay Archaeological Museum.

King Suppiluliuma, Hittite ruler *c.* 1344-1322 BCE, note spear (= power) and quill pen (= knowledge), Hatay Archaeological Museum.

King Suppiluliuma, Hittite ruler *c.* 1344-1322 BCE; note hieroglyphics at the back of statue, Hatay Archaeological Museum.

Preparation of künefe, Gaziantep.

Hişvahan Hotel in Gaziantep, a former caravanserai.

Gaziantep Castle, dating back to the Hittities, *c.* 1,650–1,180 BCE; later expanded by the Romans.

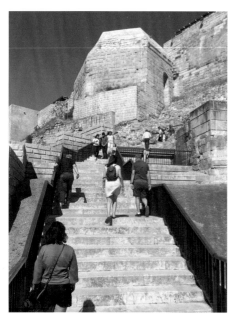

Steps leading to the top of Gaziantep Castle.

Statue of Mustafa Kemal Atatürk, founder of modern Türkiye, Gaziantep Castle Museum.

Part of Gaziantep Castle. A large section of the outer wall was destroyed in the earthquake which struck south-east Türkiye in February 2023.

Metanet Katmer Salonu (Metanet Katmer Shop) – a family-run operation, Gaziantep.

Spice shop, Gaziantep. The hanging items are sweet bell peppers.

Shoe shop, Gaziantep.

Metal worker, Gaziantep.

Gaziantep market.

Ottoman and the Hellenic observed at the
Millethan (Folk Inn), Gaziantep.

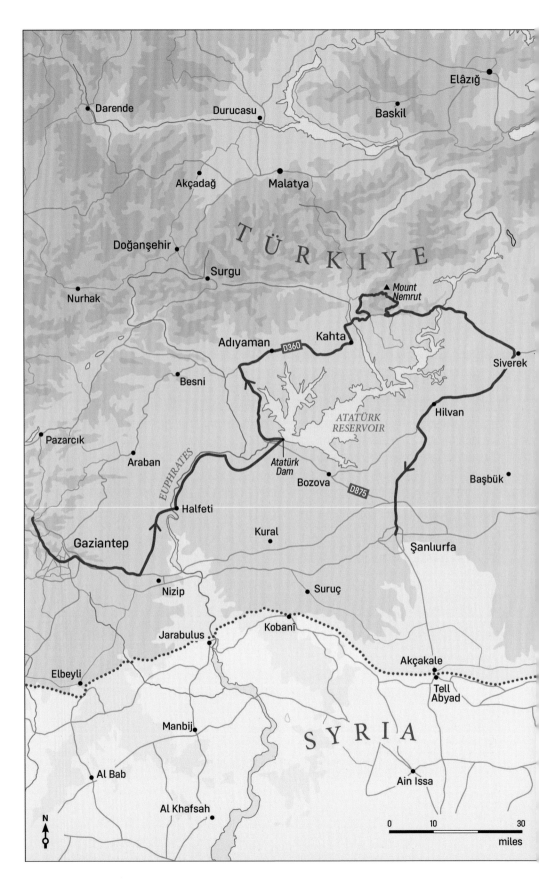

DAY 4

⊲

SUNDAY 26ᵀᴴ MAY 2019

The abiding wonder of ancient art,
the River Euphrates and Mount Nemrut

delving deep
into the past
inspires us
to venture
far into the future

PROPOSED ITINERARY:
▷ Zeugma Mosaic Museum
▷ Take a boat ride on the River Euphrates
▷ Atatürk Dam
▷ Climb Mount Nemrut by sunset
▷ Drive to Urfa

After an excellent night's sleep we were up early to be ready for a 9am departure from our comfortable Hişvahan Hotel, but before that we were served the most splendid breakfast spread where the crescent-shaped dishes in particular caught our eye.

Just as we were finishing off this sumptuous feast, Murad joined us. Although just the start of Day 4 on our north Mesopotamian adventure, it was hard to imagine that we had only met our tour guide a mere three days previously at Adana Airport. From that first meeting with Murad, our group of five had bonded well and he helped us to begin to understand the history of this part of the world. We found ourselves warming to him as conversations on numerous topics flowed effortlessly between us. I also got the feeling Murad's easy-going manner combined with a twinkle in his eye encouraged us to ask questions. And I can assure you we asked many over the course of our trip.

Our first stop of the day was the Zeugma Mosaic Museum in another part of Gaziantep and it proved to be a breathtaking experience.

The Zeugma Museum opened its doors in 2011 and it is conceived on a grand scale with 1,700 square metres of mosaics making it the largest mosaic museum in the world; bigger than the one we'd just seen in Antakya the previous day.

The numerous mosaics on display are from the ancient city of the same name, Zeugma, which was founded by Seleucia Nicator, a general from the army of Alexander the Great in the 3rd century BCE where he had the first bridge constructed over the River Euphrates. An initial settlement called Seleucia was established on the western side of the river and a pontoon bridge was erected to join up with Apamea, a community newly set up on the eastern side of the Euphrates, named after Seleucia Nicator's Persian wife. In 64 BCE, the Romans defeated Seleucid forces and took over Seleucia, changing its name to Zeugma, meaning in ancient Greek*, a 'yoking', such as a yoking of oxen, but in this case, it referred to a 'bridge [or crossing] of boats', i.e. a pontoon bridge. Zeugma was now on the eastern fringe of the Roman Empire and located in the vicinity of the other ancient kingdoms of Commagene and Osrhoene, and the Sophene, Parthian and Armenian Empires of the same period.

Under Roman rule, Zeugma – located 1,090 km (680 miles) to the south-east of modern Istanbul – prospered, becoming a city of strategic importance, both militarily and commercially, located at a key crossing of the River Euphrates where toll collections swelled the municipal coffers. This metropolis accommodated some 70,000 people with 6,000 soldiers stationed there to protect this vital garrison outpost which developed into a major trading centre for hundreds of years on the Silk Road to the Far East. Later, the city's fortunes declined and the Persian Sassanids conquered it in 253 CE, whereupon Zeugma faded from history and remained forgotten for nearly two millennia.

Recently, archaeologists had been excavating this part of Türkiye near the Euphrates where they uncovered countless artefacts from the classical world, in particular many beautiful mosaics. Similar to what we had learnt at the Hatay Museum in Antakya, however, the archaeologists were also under pressure from the Turkish government in the process of executing an ambitious river management modernisation project to enhance the supply of water to agriculture, industry and urban centres in south-eastern Anatolia. 21 dams were planned and the building of just one of them, the Birecik Dam which was constructed in 2001, meant that a large portion of the landscape which included Zeugma was due to be inundated with water. This also required the resettlement of 30,000 people (mostly Kurds) living locally in villages and towns.

Since 1995, French archaeologists working with their Turkish colleagues and others had been digging against the clock to excavate and bring to light innumerable treasures before the area became flooded with the dam construction. The archaeologists managed to gain international support – including mosaic experts from Italy – and also obtained some invaluable time extensions from the Turkish authorities to facilitate their work to rescue these gems of antiquity. With days to go before the expiry of a deadline, they managed to salvage a very rare and beautiful

Roman villa mosaic floor, for instance, now on display at the museum whereas the 14-room villa it was extracted from lies underwater.

But the inevitable came about and the waters flowed. As a result, it proved only possible to salvage a fraction of the ancient mosaics, frescoes and relics from this part of Northern Mesopotamia. Sadly, the rest of these irreplaceable artefacts were now sitting under a newly formed lake.

There was a certain irony with what was happening, in that the history of Zeugma had accumulated over a long period – centuries, in fact – whereas the uncovering of it had to be achieved in double-quick time. This prompted a lively discussion amongst our group as we debated the pros and cons of the importance of preserving what is valuable from the past in contrast to the understandable needs of the present and the future; water of course being a vital ingredient to life.

In this case, Türkiye has opted to make water more easily available to this part of the country and the people there, while also making provision for the relocation of some valuable relics to be preserved. Inevitably, though, many archaeological remains were lost. But within the well-designed contemporary setting of the Zeugma Museum, one's appreciation of past artistic wonders grew, as it was so easy to walk from one marvellous mosaic display set up in a cavernous room to the next, as the curators have endeavoured to recreate in great detail the original settings of these historic specimens from the classical world.

Even though some of these mosaics are 2,000 years old, representing mythological figures, some well known such as Mars, Dionysos, Zeus and Eros and some not so well known, for instance Oceanus, Tethys, Andromeda and Ariadne, the skill of the original creator of these works shines through. What struck me was how a mosaic could accurately convey the emotion on the face of a character shown. And the freshness of it what with its vivid colouration gave the impression that the artwork had only been created yesterday, as it were. In addition to the many mosaics depicting people, events and scenes from Latin and Greek mythology, there were also many examples of abstract designs and patterns. We also learnt that certain types of mosaic came to be used in different parts of the residence of a well-to-do family – the deity Oceanus, connected with rivers and the oceans, was to be set within a pool. More later on this topic.

Murad drew our attention to the Seal of Solomon, an ancient symbol which is reputed to date from the time of the biblical Old Testament, when King Solomon was given a ring by the Archangel Michael in response to a request from the King to be able to keep demons in check. According to legend, if the demons try to follow the direction of the lines in the two interlaced ovals, they will become confused and be condemned to an eternity of being trapped within this 'knot'.

What is fascinating about this ancient symbolic design is that Solomon's Seal (or

Knot) is highly regarded by the Jewish, Islamic and Christian religions while also finding sacred or revered application in Buddhism, and throughout Asia, Africa and Europe where Celtic art, for instance, often exhibits this distinctive emblem. Of course, there's much more to this and there are many sources of information about Solomon's Seal (or Knot) and how, for example, it is connected to the Occult and how there are a total of 44 Seals of Solomon, but let's not deviate as that is another kettle of fish altogether.

Just imagine a sun-filled scene from 2,000 years ago and the owners of a fine Roman villa on a hillside overlooking the glistening River Euphrates are seated under a canopy in their courtyard garden. Their residence would have been filled with mosaics similar to those seen at the Zeugma Museum and normally associated with how the rooms would have been used in antiquity.

A mosaic of Eros and Psyche, for example, was excavated from a leisure room while a mosaic of Oceanus and Tethys, as stated previously, was used to adorn a pool. Mosaics in rooms used for entertaining and feasting depicted mythological scenes and the striking Gypsy Girl work of art was observed on the floor of a dining room in what is now known as the Maenad Villa. This remarkable find came about through sheer happenstance as a column had fallen, thus obscuring the mosaic, and you can picture the surprise and wonder of the excavators who lifted this wayward pillar out of the way and came across the Gypsy Girl staring at them.

The maenads, by the way, were women who accompanied the god Bacchus (Roman god of wine; Dionysus was the equivalent Greek deity) and one school of thought believes that the Gypsy Girl is a maenad on account of her scarf and hooped earrings.

This mosaic is just over 78 cm (30 in) in length and 52 cm (20 in) in height.

This unique example of mosaic art is mesmerising as the eyes do seem to follow you about the room and it has been called the 'Mona Lisa of Antiquity', but of course it predates Da Vinci's masterpiece by 1,500 years.

In addition to its enigmatic allure, there is also an exciting tale about its discovery and the mysterious pathway travelled over the years leading up to the Gypsy Girl being on display in the Zeugma Museum today. Back in the 1960s, archaeological materials were unofficially excavated, even looted, then spirited out of Türkiye and some of these, including the Gypsy Girl, ended up in the United States as a result of a dubious itinerary.

Fast forward to 2011 and Bowling Green State University of Kentucky, who had purchased the Gypsy Girl mosaic in good faith, became aware that newly discovered mosaic items in Zeugma in Türkiye matched their valuable artwork on display in the Bowling Green campus. The Turkish authorities, archaeologists and their American counterparts working in cooperation with the university formulated a joint project whereby the original Gypsy Girl mosaic was to be returned to Türkiye while Turkish mosaic experts would travel to Bowling Green University and install a faithful replica there. Finally, in November 2018, this original Gypsy Girl was restored to her native land. Feray, Rashida, Suat and I were thrilled, as we realised we were so fortunate to be able to look on this wondrous work of art from the ancient world only six months after its return home.

And talking of happenstance reminds me that many historical treasures have been found by chance – here are some examples of discoveries from around the world:

▷ *New Grange, Ireland.* Prehistoric monument in County Meath with a passage tomb constructed during the Neolithic Period some 5,200 years ago, making it older than Stonehenge in England and the Egyptian pyramids. New Grange is known for the illumination of its passageways and chamber by the winter solstice sun on 21st December each year. A landowner unearthed the entrance to the tomb by chance when clearing stones on his farm in 1699.

▷ *Rosetta Stone, Egypt.* In 1799, French soldiers came across a large slab of basalt rock with mysterious writing on it when building a fort near the town of Rosetta. The script on the stone was dated back to the second century BCE and was written in three different languages: Greek, Demotic and hieroglyphics.

▷ *Venus de Milo, Greece.* This famed statue was discovered by a Greek peasant in 1820 on the island of Milos when he was looking for marble in a quarry. It is thought that this sculpture represented the Greek goddess Aphrodite and is dated to the first century BCE.

▷ *Lascaux Caves, France.* In 1940, four French teenagers were out exploring the forest by Montignac in the Dordogne area when they stumbled upon an underground cave with a huge number of drawings of animals on the walls of this subterranean area. This ancient artwork has been dated back to the Palaeolithic Period (i.e. Stone Age), some 17,000 years ago.[11]

▷ *Dead Sea Scrolls, Israel.* A group of young Bedouin goat herders in 1947 near the ancient city of Jericho came across a collection of pots containing pieces of papyrus with what appeared to be old writing. Being unaware of the significance of their chance find, they sold the papyrus artefacts to a local dealer for a pittance but later the value of these scrolls increased immeasurably when scholars determined that they were the earliest known biblical writings.

▷ *Derinkuyu, Türkiye*. In Cappadocia, a man was renovating his house in 1963 when he uncovered a huge network of underground tunnels beneath his home. It turned out that he had stumbled upon a vast subterranean settlement (constructed some 2,800 years ago) which could accommodate up to 20,000 people living underground.

▷ *Terracotta Army, China*. In 1979, a group of Chinese farmers were digging a well when they chanced upon a buried statue which they thought was an old Buddha sculpture. Long story short, it proved to be a remarkable discovery as some 8,000 life-sized terracotta warriors along with their horses and chariots were uncovered. Reportedly, they date back to the 3rd century BCE during the reign of the Emperor Qin Shi Huang.

▷ *Cave Art, Indonesia*. On an island in Sulawesi in 2017, an Australian archaeologist reported that his colleague, after climbing a tree, had discovered a cave passage with ancient art on the walls depicting a buffalo hunting scene. This incredible artistic find has been estimated to be 44,000 years old.

I find it amazing that these worldwide examples of great historical importance were all chance finds in the same way that the Gypsy Girl of Zeugma was unearthed. It never ceases to astound me how much of our knowledge today has come down to us through the ages by means of fluke discovery.

Since we'd been admiring mosaics and all their finery while learning the stories associated with them at two major museums in Antakya and Gaziantep, our small group then learnt about what a mosaic is actually made of. Mosaics are produced from a variety of rocks with different natural colours and then broken up into very small pieces called *tesserae* for insertion into the overall design of the mosaic. They are called *tesserae* (plural) on account of the four-sided nature of each mosaic piece – *tessara* (τέσσερα) being the Greek word for the numeral 4. The dimensions of a *tessara* (singular) are usually equal in size to a person's fingernail.

Our guide Murad pointed out that the mosaics excavated in Zeugma fall into two broad categories: Greek and Roman. The ancient Greek mosaics are based on figures and events from classical mythology whereas the later Roman ones break with this tradition by depicting ordinary people, with a further development being the use of abstract geometric design.

We noted from a number of the mosaics and frescoes seen, that there was 'layering' involved due to different art works being laid down successively in the same location, i.e. one mosaic or fresco exactly on top of another older one.

This being a Turkish museum, I thought it fitting to quote from Turkish Nobel Literary Laureate, Orhan Pamuk: "Real museums are places where Time is transformed into Space," from his book, *The Museum of Innocence*, 2006.

We departed Gaziantep at about 1.40pm, driving along the D-52 highway for an hour and a half until we reached the small farming and fishing town of Halfeti on the eastern banks of the Euphrates. Owing to the construction of the Birecik Dam, as mentioned previously, the original community of Halfeti along with other villages and towns locally were now under water.

My research showed me that Halfeti had existed since its foundation by the Neo Assyrian King Shalmaneser III almost 3,000 years ago. Before the dam was completed in the 1990s, the population of some 2,000 people were relocated safely to higher ground in what is now called 'New Halfeti' but still in close proximity to their perennial source of water, the River Euphrates.

River Euphrates – a glistening turquoise thread of water meandering through the Mesopotamian Plain

I've known rivers:

> I've known rivers ancient as the world and older than
> the flow of human blood in human veins.
> My soul has grown deep like the rivers.
> I bathed in the Euphrates when dawns were young.
>
> …
>
> I've known rivers:
> Ancient, dusky rivers.
> My soul has grown deep like the rivers.
>
> Langston Hughes, *The Negro Speaks of Rivers*, 1926

We stopped momentarily at a place that was the perfect viewing point overlooking Halfeti and the river. We emerged from the air-conditioned coolness of our bus and all four of us stood blinking in the bright afternoon sun gazing down at the dark turquoise-coloured, full-bodied river only a short distance away. But this was not any old river, this was the Euphrates, with all its legendary connotations and biblical connections. There was silence as the four of us took in this amazing view. A sense of wonder hung in the air as we realised that we were looking at this ancient waterway for the first time in our lives. I mentally pinched myself at being able to take in the significance of a river that I'd only ever read or heard about since I was a lad growing up in Ireland. I remember my father bringing books home from Trinity College Dublin Library and showing me pictures of this river of historical importance. But now, decades later, as I was standing on the promontory looking out over the river, it struck me this was not a still picture that I as a ten-year old was looking at, but instead more than half a century had zipped by and I'm now a 65-year-old man gazing in childlike astonishment at the sight of the actual Euphrates.

Don't forget the River Euphrates is revered by Jews, Muslims and Christians, as it is mentioned in the holy writings of the Talmud, the Hadith and the Bible respectively: this river is very much part of the essence of the three Abrahamic religions and was also an essential element of earlier (but now extinct) civilisations and belief systems that had existed in this part of the world. The river runs through everything and yet is a constant: people and their convictions may come and go but the river is still there.

We took some photos of this momentary 'pit-stop' by Halfeti and the River Euphrates to record this memorable occasion.

The gods dug out the Tigris river (bed)
And then dug out the Euphrates.

Atrahasis I, Tablet 1
Myths from Mesopotamia, 3,800 BP◊
Creation, The Flood, Gilgamesh, and Others by Stephanie Dalley.
◊BP – Before Present, i.e. 3,800 years before the present day; similar to BCE below.

A river flowed out of Eden to water the garden, and there it divided and became
four rivers. The name of the first is the Pishon. It is the one that flowed around
the whole land of Havilah, where there is gold. And the gold of that land is good;
bdellium and onyx stone are there. The name of the second river is the Gihon. It is
the one that flowed around the whole land of Cush. And the name of the third river
is the Tigris, which flows east of Assyria. And the fourth river is the Euphrates.

Genesis 2:10-14

The Euphrates river is the master of all rivers in this world and in the Hereafter.

Imam Ali

revered River Euphrates
flowing through history
shows us
how to speak with love
to the future

Euphrates is the longest river in western Asia at circa 2,700 km (1,700 miles). In texts from the third millennium BCE from Mari (ancient state in present-day Syria) the river occurs as a deity. From its sources in north-east Türkiye, the river takes a southerly course into northern Syria, where it turns south-east and flows into the

Persian Gulf after joining the Tigris. According to Genesis 2:14, the Euphrates was one of the four branches of the river which rises in Eden to water the garden of Eden. The Euphrates – also called "The River" or "The Great River" (see below) – forms the northern boundary of the ideal land promised to Israel (Genesis 15:18; Deuteronomy 11:24; Joshua 1:4). The river is also referred to in Jeremiah 51:60–64, when Jeremiah instructed Seraiah upon reaching Babylon to read the prophecies of Jeremiah, bind them with a stone and cast them into the Euphrates as a sign of the imminent destruction of that city. Naturally, a great many cities were built on or near the banks of the Euphrates; among the best known are Carchemish, Mari, Babylon, Erech and Ur, known from biblical and cuneiform sources; and Pumbedita, Nehardea, Mata Mehasya and Sura, known from the Babylonian Talmud.[12]

Early that Sunday afternoon in late May 2019, as we awaited the departure of our boat on the River Euphrates, we were serenaded by a well turned-out gentleman and his violin. I mean what's more normal than listening to stringed melodies that waft through the air as you sip on a refreshing lemon drink and look out over the waters of a river that's been known since the dawn of civilisation?

We boarded our river vessel, named the 'Bl. Manavgat' (Bl. = Belediye, i.e. Municipality of Manavgat, a town near Antalya). The boat was a large craft with two tiers of viewing platforms, shaded thank goodness. Just before we set off from

Our Halfeti violinist serenading us prior to sailing on the Euphrates

Halfeti, the crew of the Bl. Manavgat decided that their passengers were in need of further musical entertainment and the loudspeakers began to blast out at high volume local Turkish songs and traditional music. We set off from the marina and travelled upstream, passing the ancient site of Rumkale (means Roman Castle in Turkish) where the ruins of an old fort are perched on a strategic strongpoint overlooking the river, dating way back to the Assyrians and in turn occupied by successive conquerors including the Greeks, Romans, Armenians and Mamluks.

Further upriver, we saw the old town of Halfeti, now half-submerged, with only the minaret of the now-hidden mosque visible above the waters. Nearby, we could see many deserted houses dotting the hillside.

As described before, the construction of the Birecik Dam caused the region to be flooded as part of a mammoth river management undertaking (the South-eastern Anatolia Project) that helped to improve water supply to this part of the country. This huge scheme was first mooted in the 1950s, and over the following 60 years, extensive work has been carried out in six provinces of Anatolia encompassing 70,000 square kilometres (27,000 square miles), which in turn has brought about the completion of 22 dams (including the Birecik and Atatürk dams), 19 hydroelectricity stations and many other infrastructure improvements. This dam-building project was on a massive scale as some 55,000 people had to be safely relocated from more than 100 villages to new communities before the area was flooded.

From our river boat vantage point as we sailed through the calm waters of the Euphrates, we saw the remnants of further abandoned villages on the hillsides we passed.

We returned to Halfeti after two hours and, on disembarking, Murad suggested we try some of the local gözleme – a traditional Turkish flatbread that can be savoury or sweet depending on the ingredients used. In what can be best described as a makeshift riverside café, where our gözleme was prepared and served, the wee feast proved to be really delicious, which we enjoyed with a cup of tea. We agreed our boat journey on the River Euphrates would now be considered a precious memory and then Murad expanded further on his (tongue-in-cheek) philosophy of how civilisation changes and develops on account of men acceding to the wishes of women, with his QED killer argument proving, he averred, that women are, therefore, the superior sex. Naturally, this prompted much discussion which continued on the days following and throughout the remainder of our trip.

We also learned that near Rumkale there is a 12th-century church, named after St Nerses, and the Barşavma Monastery dating back 700 years.

Of particular note, 72 km (45 miles) further downstream of the River Euphrates on the Turkish-Syrian frontier lies the ancient site of Carchemish (Karkamiş in Turkish) dating back 5,000 years to the Neolithic Period. Occupied by different groups of people including the Mittani, Hittites and Neo-Assyrian empires, Carchemish is familiar to scholars of the ancient world, as this place is mentioned not only in the Bible but also other texts from prehistory. It is a major site of archaeological importance with 60 per cent of the area on the Turkish side of the border and the remaining 40 per cent in Syria. British historical figure Lawrence of Arabia carried out excavations in Carchemish over a three-year period from 1912–14.

The River Euphrates has inspired many stories and legends. The most celebrated of these is *The Epic of Gilgamesh*.

Ut-napishtim spoke to him, to Gilgamesh,
'Let me reveal to you a closely guarded matter, Gilgamesh,
And let me tell you the secret of the gods.
Shuruppak is a city you yourself know,
Situated (on the bank of) the Euphrates.

That city was already old when the gods within it
Decided that the great gods should make a flood.

Gilgamesh XI [Tablet XI] Myths from Mesopotamia, 3,800 BP
Creation, The Flood, Gilgamesh, and Others by Stephanie Dalley, 2008

Since I've been referring to Gilgamesh in company with other illustrious characters and dramatic events of long ago, perhaps it might be a good idea to explore this ancient saga from this place, Mesopotamia.

The Epic of Gilgamesh, a Sumerian poem written on clay tablets in cuneiform* script, is considered to be the oldest known work of literature dating back 4,000 years. It predates Homer's *The Iliad* by one and a half millennia and the Sumerian epic has influenced the famous Greek poem and other major works from antiquity. The story is about the life of Gilgamesh, king of Uruk, who is two-thirds divine as he is the son of a mother who is a goddess, and a father who is a king-cum-priest. Gilgamesh is a complex but flawed character endowed with superhuman powers, and in possession of good looks, intelligence and courage. But he is also impulsive, arrogant and insensitive to others. In addition, his treatment of women would certainly have him on the wrong side of the #MeToo movement of today. The poem follows Gilgamesh as he sets out on a quest seeking the prize of immortality following the death of his close friend, Enkidu. Gilgamesh has many adventures while coming into contact with a host of characters along the way and he does undergo an arc of development in the traditional narrative sense based on the numerous experiences he has.

This epic poem touches on universal themes which could apply in any period of time, including that of the 21st century: the role of a leader; life and death; camaraderie among men and relationships between men and women; life in the country as opposed to the city and also the role of civilisation. If interested in the way the verses are written, then it is worth pointing out that *The Epic of Gilgamesh* is written in a metre known as hexameter – a compositional style with six stressed syllables per line commonly used in classical poetry. Now, the jury's out on the desirability of this form of metre as, on the one hand, this construct of sound regularity when read aloud can create a sense of musicality or rhythm which bobs you along as the tale unfolds. On the other hand, however, the reader or listener may feel hemmed in by the constant use of the hexameter structure, as it can give the poem a rigid or formulaic 'feel'. Let the reader be the judge.

Spoiler Alert: this epic poem concludes with Gilgamesh, despite his best attempts, being unable to achieve eternal existence and he is shown coming to terms with his own mortality. His character improves as he matures and develops an awareness of his place in the world while also becoming more compassionate as a king who cares for the people under him. Gilgamesh then attempts to create a legacy that will carry his good name a long way into the future after his demise.

*The Epic of Gilgamesh** could be considered a morality tale on a grand scale that is thousands of years old while possessing a golden nugget quality from the story-telling perspective: it is ageless.

Atatürk Dam – an incredible feat of river engineering

Leaving Halfeti behind us, after a 40-minute drive, we stopped at an elevated point where we could get a decent view of the Atatürk Dam. As stated previously, this enormous barrage complex is part of a government hydro-electric programme which has involved the construction of many dams (including the one we saw) on the Euphrates and Tigris rivers.

Historical sites also were inundated such as the ancient town of Samosata (Samsat), the capital of the ancient Commagene kingdom. Afterwards, a new town with the same name, Samsat, was established to accommodate the 2,000 inhabitants displaced from this particular area.

Geopolitical Developments

A further consideration with the construction of the Atatürk Dam on the River Euphrates was that two of Türkiye's neighbours, Syria and Iraq, became greatly concerned that the former was using its control of the waters upriver within its territory as a means of either deliberately reducing or holding back on the water supply (which Türkiye denies) – and this was despite various agreements and treaties dating back to 1946 on the acceptable use of the water of the Euphrates by the three nations concerned. Türkiye, on the other hand, has disagreed while maintaining that with the construction of the Atatürk Dam, the flow of the Euphrates is now more evenly spread throughout the year, reducing the risk of flooding and drought, thus generating more reliable water supplies in spite of seasonal variations.

By the way, the name of Ut-napishtim – also recorded as Uta-naishtim – quoted above in Gilgamesh XI is thought to be the Akkadian forerunner of Noah, as in Noah and the Ark. According to some ancient scholars of this period of history, Noah is a (corrupted) abbreviation arising from the elision of the prefix 'Uta' and the suffix 'tim', thus leaving 'Naish' which then morphed into 'Noah'. These ancient Akkadian tablets from far-off Babylonian times record not only one flood but many over the millennia and it would appear also these floods were a regular feature of life. So, the story is told that one ruler some 5,000 years ago ordered that all the official records and the library in his city of Assur (now in modern Iraq) by the River Tigris were to be copied and that these copies were then to be transported to another city, Uruk, for safety and out of harm's way of any floods. It would appear, then, risk management was well practised in 3,000 BCE!

In addition to the evidence pointing to the regularity of flooding in Mesopotamia, there are also indications that these floods, when they did happen in antiquity, were localised events within parts of a kingdom or an empire rather than the engulfing of the entire planet and threatening all of human civilisation as the biblical tale in Genesis 6-9 recounts. Some scholars in this field of religious studies have suggested that the story of Noah and the Ark may have been acquired from ancient Assyrian sources – recorded in Akkadian cuneiform tablets dating back 5,000 years (please note the Assyrian origins of the word Noah as described above) – where also the details of more than one flood had become amalgamated into a single account of an event that then was written up as gospel in the Bible – please excuse the unintentional pun, honest guv.

⌖ Mount Nemrut (Nimrod) – Nemrut Daği

Tempus fugit on this Day 4 of our trip and we departed from the Atatürk Dam about 6ish and set off for our next destination, Mount Nemrut (a mountain 2,164 m [7,100 ft] in height) threading our way through narrow rural roads that were often hilly, but we were grateful as our driver was familiar with the area and drove quickly but safely. The aim was to reach this mountain and then get to the summit in time to enjoy sunset scheduled for 8.15pm later that same evening. There was to be no let-up for us travelling folks.

En route to the mountain, not far from the city of Kâhta, we shoehorned a visit to see a very well-preserved Roman bridge, nearly 2,000 years old, spanning the River Cendere. Originally constructed for military purposes by the Roman general and later emperor, Septimus Severus, it is 118 m (387 ft) long and until quite recently was used for vehicular traffic until the building of a modern bridge nearby. Standing as we did on this modern bridge, we gazed in awe at the ancient bridge a short distance away. Judging by its perfect arch and the three surviving Doric columns, the Romans certainly knew a thing or two about longevity in architecture.

We then sped on to Mount Nemrut and, at base camp, with that engaging expression of his, Murad was off and away, charging up the path leading to the top. Don't forget that our guide had been fasting since dawn and yet was still carrying on with the strength of a Trojan and giving us chapter and verse on all the marvellous places we were passing through, plus he was conscientiously responding with good humour to boot to all the questions Suat and I were bombarding him with – I mean, some of these foreign tourists just don't know when to ease off! Onwards and upwards we climbed with some of us – the author noticeably – puffing and panting on the way up.

Our way to the top was a combination of walking, two separate bus rides and then a final hoof up to the summit to catch the sunset. The five of us set off on our ascent but Suat quickly took the lead while Murad encouraged the slow coaches (i.e. Feray, Rashida and me) to keep moving.

The second bus deposited us at the uppermost base camp, as it were, and Murad announced that we'd have to step on it if we were to make sunset in time. Fortunately, there was a fine-looking pathway chiselled into the side of the mountain which made the final leg of our climb not too arduous. As we neared the summit, the temperature dropped and we were glad that we'd remembered to bring warm clothing with us. Suitably kitted out, we climbed apace with renewed spirits.

Our efforts were richly rewarded, I am thrilled to confirm, as our band of four and Murad reached the very pinnacle of Mount Nemrut with about 10 minutes to spare before sundown. We were surprised to see quite a crowd at the top as they must have climbed ahead of us. We all awaited the final *denouement* of the sun slipping beneath the far-off horizon on this beautifully clear evening, casting its dramatic orange glow over the Mesopotamian landscape. We had to watch our step in a few places, though, as there was snow and ice about.

Mount Nemrut – why is it so called?

Nemrut (Nimrod), as I'm sure you'll recall from your religious studies, was the son of Cush, who was the grandson of Noah, which meant that Nemrut was the great grandson of the venerable person who had the Ark. Nemrut is mentioned in the Bible (Books of Genesis and Chronicles), in Jewish Scripture and is referenced in the Qur'an when an epic battle took place between Solomon (Suleyman) and a 'king' – the latter has been understood to be Nemrut.

It has proved extremely difficult to evidence the actual existence of Nemrut and ancient stories describe him as a king and a mighty hunter in Shinar. Furthermore, it has been conjectured that Nemrut is an amalgam of several characters from Mesopotamian and Akkadian antiquity. In the Talmud, the Land of Shinar is Mesopotamia and could be a linguistic corruption of either of two Hebrew phrases meaning two rivers, '*shene neharof*' or two cities, '*shene arim*'. Nemrut is also associated with the well-known story of the construction of the Tower of Babel, and where he exhibited a rebellious nature disputing the word of God, thus leading to the Almighty creating many languages.

At the top of the mountain is the grave of Antiochus, supposedly in the large tumulus or burial mound some 46 m (150 ft) high, although his actual grave remains undiscovered to this day. Antiochus was the son of Mithratis and married to a person of Hellenic and Persian blood, Princess Isias Philostorgos of Cappadocia.

With their union, Antiochus and his queen not only bridged the two worlds of ancient Greece and Persia politically when they became rulers of the Commagene Empire – which sat in what is now south-eastern Türkiye – but they also helped to unite both their peoples in a spiritual sense when they established the Commagene religion which was a fusion of the Hellenic and Persian pagan belief systems. While being an imaginative and positive way of uniting people religiously, scholars of this era believe that it may have also been a political manoeuvre to maintain social unity within the kingdom.

On the top of Mount Nemrut there were plenty of artefacts to see but the most striking examples were the many statuary heads some 2.1–2.4 m (7–8 ft) high representing figures of mythology and antiquity. The heads are thought to have been part of much larger seated statues which had been transported to the summit around the reign of Antiochus but that they had been 'beheaded' at some point in the past, due possibly to religious or political difference or iconoclasm. Because of its importance historically, Mount Nemrut was declared a UNESCO World Heritage site in 1987.

Excavations and research point to Antiochus attempting to create a system of belief that would outlive his natural life and he worked to make Mount Nemrut an important religious centre with links to Zoroastrianism – hence the many statues and monuments visible on the mountain top to this day. This served as a heady catalyst for further inquiry on our part, as the eternal flame of curiosity was being fanned by this exploration of not only the past but also so much more. This prompted the quartet to discuss the Zoroastrian belief system, while reflecting that it was a very old religion dating back 4,000 years where the core tenets are based on the "threefold path of good thoughts, good words and good deeds". In contemporary terms, Freddie Mercury, the late lead singer of the British pop group Queen, was a Parsi and therefore a member of the Zoroastrian faith.

Later on, when writing about all of this, the vision of a snowy Mount Nemrut and the breathtaking views from the summit lingered in my brain and, for some reason, made me think of the American literary figure Sylvia Plath and her book *The Bell Jar*, where she writes about an episode in an area of snow-covered mountains: "The cold air punished my lungs and sinuses to a visionary clearness."

And then my mind moved onto a heart-warming memory from Ireland the previous year, in September 2018, when I had travelled there with my wife and the two same friends, Feray and Suat. We had gone to County Sligo and had climbed the 305 m (1,000 ft) hill called Knocknarea overlooking the seaside town of Strandhill and the Atlantic Ocean. According to Irish mythology, Queen Maeve is said to be interred in a tumulus 10 m (33 ft) high on the top of Knocknarea and is believed to date from 3,000 BCE. Archaeologists have cited evidence of this hilltop being a place where pagan religious ceremonies were held and even blood sacrifice.

The cairn enclosing the tomb of Queen Maeve seen at the summit of Knocknarea, Sligo, Ireland.

On reflection, there are many other examples to be gleaned from ancient legends and mythologies, belief systems, cultures, art and literature, and geographically dispersed locations around the world where mountains serve as emotional, spiritual and life-affirming sustenance, and on this occasion Mount Nemrut had definitely played its role in this regard.

What is it about mountains and their unique environment that affects people and always attracts interest?

On a small personal note, in my research to try and ensure all historical references are accurate, I've come across more than one Antiochus, Seleucus et al., so I've endeavoured to quote the correct personage applicable at a given point in this travelogue and if any errors have crept in, they are the sole responsibility of the author.

In the cool mountain air as the sunlight faded just before we descended from on high, I heard our tour guide in earnest conversation with Feray, Rashida and Suat. Even though I was standing a little bit away from them, I could make out that Murad was carefully and knowledgeably answering questions being put to him about Nemrut and the many historical figures associated with this special place. Murad's openness to and encouragement of our quartet's inquiring minds took me back momentarily to my undergrad days at Trinity where the practice of 'making you think' was the norm. Questions of any kind could be posed which challenged all manner of received ideas, encouraging you to step outside your comfort zone.

There was no hiding place and the same rules applied to the very same lecturers, tutors and professors who propounded this way of thinking and dealing with ideas. Needless to say, this paved the way for an invigorating and thought-provoking time as a student at university back in the 1970s and I relished every moment of it where freedom of speech was fully exercised and also fully respected. Within a very wide latitude of reason, there were no limits to what was open for exploration, scrutiny and discussion.

And talking of questions reminds me of a wee anecdote from my first year as a student. I was friends with a chap reading philosophy who later went on to become a clergyman and he recounted how he had handled an exam question in his given subject. The question was – "Is this a question?" Having studied the course, where they had touched on many philosophical ideas and concepts dating from the classical period (Socrates) up to the modern era (Wittgenstein), it was expected that the students should present a well-argued and detailed answer demonstrating not only their understanding of the material covered but also to include some of their own thinking, thus covering several handwritten foolscap pages.

My friend's written response was succinct to put it mildly. "If this is a question, then this is an answer", as if echoing Descartes' famous terse maxim, "*Cogito ergo sum*" (I think therefore I am). My friend passed and later graduated with full honours.

Brevity can be effective, *n'est-ce pas?*

do questions
always
need answers
or, are they stepping stones
to clearer thinking?

Meanwhile, back in the real world at Mount Nemrut, the sun had finally set and we'd taken oodles of photos at the top of this historic mountain while admiring the panoramic views. I pondered on the movers and shakers of this now ancient Commagene civilisation that was positioned among the Roman, Sophene and Osrhoene Empires with the Parthian and Georgian kingdoms nearby. As mentioned on a previous page, under the rule of King Antiochus Theos and his wife, Queen Isias Philostorgos of Cappadocia, a new belief system was established called the Commagene religion, which was a fusion of Hellenistic and Persian belief systems. What had inspired them to go about constructing a place of worship to their new faith with all these enormous statues on top of a mountain?

This mammoth undertaking had to be initially visualised, designed, then finally constructed and it would have needed many people to complete this work. It is not known whether the large statues themselves could have been carved and chiselled out elsewhere and then hauled up the mountainside or whether they had been sculpted or bashed into shape *in situ* at the top of the mountain but, in either case, some poor sods in antiquity, slave labour no doubt, would have had to drag these heavy and cumbersome stone objects 2,130 m (7,000 ft) up to the summit. Not a pleasant task that last one. Gradually, the temple would have taken shape, the statues finished to reflect this new creed.

So out of all this energy expenditure in terms of imagination, design, labour and even travails of the past millennia, we were able to catch a glimpse of that era of long ago.

As we made our way down the mountain, I pondered on the civilisations we had heard about associated with Antiochus Theos and Isias Philostorgos of Cappadocia: Commagene, Sophene, Osrhoene, Parthian, Georgian and, of course, Roman. While they would have flourished in the past some 2,000 years ago, none of these civilisations had survived up to the present day. Why?

In a way, this line of inquiry links up with a question I had posed on Day 3: are civilisations finite? That's a "toughie" as a friend of mine with an encyclopaedic knowledge of pop music who worked in a Dublin record store used to say, but I'll attempt an answer.

As far as I can see, I would suggest civilisations are finite: they come into existence and then at some point later on, they come to an end. No civilisation I can think of has endured. The duration of a civilisation may be governed by a number of factors, such as the strength or quality of internal structures like governance and leadership, workable systems of law, defence, finance, health and education and, of course, an underlying ethos and belief system (or systems) the population can accept and have faith in. But history demonstrates clearly that no matter how robust or long-lasting a civilisation has been, there comes a time when they go into decline and, at some point, cease to exist or are taken over by a newcomer civilisation.

What does that mean for contemporary human civilisation?

Let's return to the evening descent from the top of Mount Nemrut. The ever-trustworthy Suat had very thoughtfully carried a bag of food and water for Murad to break his fast at the summit but our tour guide preferred to wait till we reached base camp further down. In fact, as we got there, we could hear the *Maghrib* evening prayer call signifying the conclusion of fasting at sunset. We all joined Murad in having delicious lentil soup with freshly baked bread served at the restaurant which was busy with many of the people who had also climbed this mountain.

summit climbed
an echo
of youth
rising free
with hope

We were very happy bunnies as we piled onto our bus and drove towards Şanlıurfa/
Urfa via Adiyaman taking the D-360 highway at first and then turning onto the
D-875, a journey of 190 km (120 miles). As we sped along, the others nodded off
in the darkness – not surprising really, as we'd had such a packed day. But my mind
couldn't rest and I marvelled at the whole experience so far. This odyssey of ours
was turning out to be an incredible opportunity to learn about past civilisations,
how they lived and how they recorded their history in various ways: their buildings,
monuments, statues, artefacts and legends, in some cases with a written record on
ancient clay tablets, many of which have survived to this day.

As from the start of our mammoth trip, I'd been making copious notes in my
notebook (*Some Shit To Remember*, remember) and began jotting down what
we'd done over the course of Day 4. As I came to the end of my scribblings, or
so I thought, Murad, who was sitting in the front seat of the minibus next to the
driver, must have read my thoughts as he turned around and grinning said that
the day wasn't over yet. Our guide said that when we reached the hotel, he would
recommend where to go for dinner.

Later, the lights of Urfa came into my sleepy vision as our driver entered the city.
The others began to stir into semi-wakefulness and Suat turned to me asking, "How
much have you scribbled in your little notebook, Nicholas?"

"Twelve pages so far, Suat," was my reply.

We pulled up at our hotel, the Şehrazat/Sherazade, and said our goodbyes to
Murad. It was just after 11pm. After checking in and refreshing ourselves, we were
out again on the streets on the hunt for a lateish dinner. It felt as if the night was
just beginning. Even at this hour, the place was buzzing, being Ramadan, and while
exploring the old town we came across a square where people were milling about.
A guy from a restaurant approached us, inviting us to look at his menu. We liked
what was on offer and took a seat at some rough-and-ready, village-type wooden
tables and benches in an open square where other diners were enjoying their meal.
Eating *en plein air* seemed ideal as the prevailing temperature was so benign.

As we sat down, we noticed that there were bowls full of fresh vegetables and salad
on the table. What was unexpected were the bowls of unpeeled raw onions next to
chopping boards and sharp knives. On seeing this display, Suat exclaimed, "Oh look,
Nicholas, your favourite!" He was being sarcastic of course, well aware that I'm not
fond of raw onions. It seemed though that onions 'with everything' was a culinary
norm in Urfa and so we went with the flow.

Local custom dictates that in Urfa, restaurant diners cut and prepare their own
vegetables and shallots to accompany the main courses served to them. When the
waiters brought the various dishes we had ordered to the table, we had some fun

chopping up our greens and salads to go with our meals. We were well fed and ready to hit the town.

To satisfy our sweet tooth, therefore, we went in search of a *pastane* (pastry-cum-sweet shop) as Feray told us that she couldn't possibly return home to the UK without first trying the konefe and kadaif that her sister had recommended was a must in Urfa. It was just the ticket when we came across a small café with outdoor seating on the pavement serving this delicious dessert. As we polished off this final dinner course, we continued to see the hustle and bustle carrying on late into the small hours with people of all ages out and about.

For foodies: konefe is a traditional dessert made with shredded filo pastry soaked in rosewater syrup and then layered with cheese, almonds and pistachios. Kadaif, on the other hand, is in the form of noodles covered with butter and pistachio and then baked until golden brown. It is served with lemon sugar syrup and traditional kaymak cream – similar to clotted cream.

By this stage, we were very well fed and even we young people agreed that our energy levels were starting to sag, so we hailed a taxi and returned to our hotel close to 3am. Best to hit the sack as Murad had promised us an early start at 9am later the same day!

---

*Ancient Greek
Roman soldiers, municipal leaders and the inhabitants of Zeugma and other cities of the Roman Empire at this period often used (ancient) Greek as a *lingua franca*.

*Cuneiform
From the Latin meaning 'wedge-shaped'. Cuneiform script first appeared some 4,000+ years ago in Sumer (in the area known as Mesopotamia, now situated in southern Iraq) and was produced by pressing a stylus (made from a reed growing on the banks of a river) into soft, damp clay. This was then allowed to dry and a hardened clay tablet with cuneiform writing on it was the result. Tablets varied in size from one that could fit into the palm of your hand to much larger examples used for public notices.
In my research on cuneiform, I came across a website which translates contemporary writing into Assyrian cuneiform.[13] And using this to translate my name 'Nicholas' into cuneiform results in:

*The Epic of Gilgamesh
Since I've attempted to adopt a global view of civilisation, I thought I'd look into other heroic or epic tales from long ago emanating from other places in the world and I came across an extensive list of 99.[14] As an Irishman, I noted six of these ancient sagas have a connection to my homeland, including Cycle of the Gods, the Ulster Cycle and Táin Bó Cúailnge.

The covered entrance to the Zeugma Mosaic Museum, Gaziantep.

Murad describing the Seal of Solomon – two interlinked ovals at the centre of this concentric design, Zeugma Mosaic Museum.

Interior of Zeugma Mosaic Museum.

Mosaic depicting Dionysos (shown centre), accompanied by Telete (left) and Skyrtos (right); Zeugma Mosaic Museum.

Tethys, a goddess of mythology, daughter of Uranus and Gaia, sister and husband of Oceanus, Zeugma Mosaic Museum.

Mosaic with abstract design, 3rd century CE – probably Roman, Zeugma Mosaic Museum.

Mosaic with abstract design, 3rd century CE – probably Roman, Zeugma Mosaic Museum.

Interior scene showing realistic recreation of original location where mosaic was found; Zeugma Mosaic Museum.

Gypsy Girl of Zeugma, a 2,000-year old mosaic, Zeugma Mosaic Museum.

The River Euphrates, showing the new town of Halfeti in the middle distance.

Rumkale (Roman Castle ruins) seen on the River Euphrates.

Part-submerged town of Old Halfeti on the River Euphrates.

The Atatürk Dam, on the River Euphrates, the third largest dam in the world, Adıyaman – Şanlıurfa.

Standing by the River Euphrates. Pictured left to right are Suat, Feray, Rashida and Nicholas.

A Kodak moment on our boat on the River Euphrates.

Not far from Mount Nemrut, there is a well-preserved Roman bridge nearly 2,000 years old spanning the River Cendere near the city of Kâhta.

Mount Nemrut, 2,134 m (7,000 ft) high, in the Taurus Mountains, famed for the many statues on the summit.

Ascent of Mount Nemrut.

Statuesque head of King Antiochus, atop Mount Nemrut.

View from Mount Nemrut.

Sunset over Mount Nemrut, showing the many heads of statues at the summit.

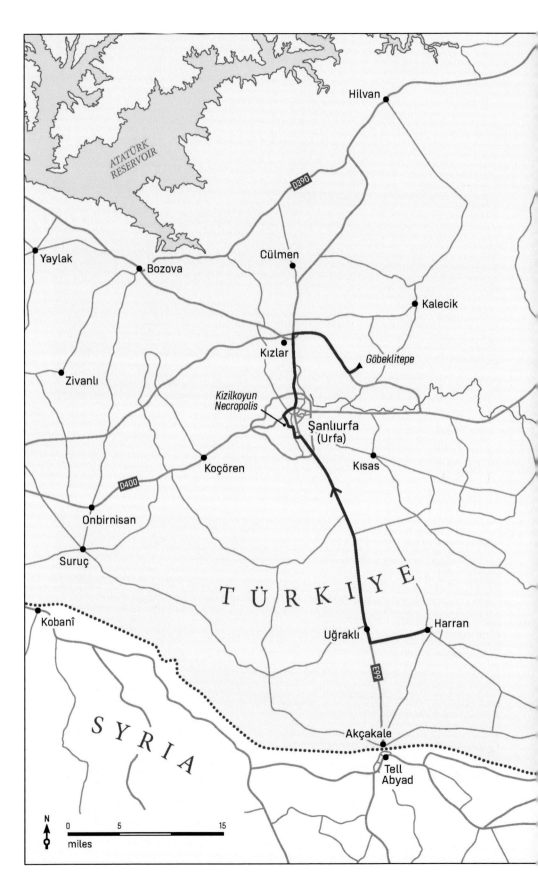

MONDAY 27ᵀᴴ MAY 2019

Piecing together a picture of the distant past

histories
from afar
help us
better understand
our existence

PROPOSED ITINERARY:
▷ Drive to Harran and Urfa Archaeological Museum
▷ View Kizilkoyun Necropolis (Red Sheep City of the Dead)
▷ Urfa Mosaic Museum
▷ Hotel El Ruha Grotto
▷ Explore Göbeklitepe (Pot Bellied Hill), unique archaeological site
▷ Urfa: Nightlife

> … About 6 started for Harran. No incidents, country everywhere as flat as possible; only huge tells about every two miles; crossed one small stream soon after mid-way. Much mirage: tried to photograph one pool but failed: nothing shown on the ground-glass. The tower of Harran cathedral was in sight for four hours: all elongated by the mirage, it becked and bobbed in the most fantastic way, now shivering from top to bottom, now bowing to left or right, now a deep curtsey forward. Day very hot and drank five bottles of water between 6 and 2.30: did not stop anywhere on the way. … Many camels. Plain all wet and very fertile. Dhurra, liquorice, barley and corn.
>
> The Diary of 1911, Monday, July 17; T.E. Lawrence; from *The Essential T.E. Lawrence*, 1951

Quite rightly given our chock-full itinerary, our guide liked to have us out on the road from a decent hour after a decent breakfast. Not quite as early as our fellow explorer of old above, Lawrence of Arabia, who you might recall was in this parish just over a century ago carrying out archaeological work in areas of interest connected with the ancient Hittite Empire in present-day southern Türkiye, Iraq and Syria – i.e. Mesopotamia. Lawrence also had an opportunity to spend some time in what is today a province of northern Saudi Arabia and even ventured further south to Jeddah on the Red Sea coast in the early part of the 20th century. Much later, Suat, Rashida and I had lived and worked there in the 1980s and 90s. I remember well seeing an old-style, grand-looking building in the centre of the *al balad* of Jeddah (i.e. the city centre) locally referred to as 'Lawrence's House', where he is reputed to have stayed. It was a fairly large building along the lines of a merchant's white-walled villa, with lattice windows and chiselled woodwork frames. It was obviously kept in good nick as it always appeared so when I was in the vicinity but, sadly, I never saw its interior as it was never open to the public.

The *tell* that Lawrence mentions in his diary entry about Harran is a derivation of the Arabic word, *tall*, meaning small hill or mound, and refers to how the landscape changes and is rendered 'hilly' when the debris from countless generations builds up, thus forming such mounds of artefacts which turn out to be archaeological manna from heaven when searching out relics from the past. Dhurra, by the way, is another word for sorghum, a member of the grass family, used for the production of foodstuffs and distilling.

And since we're talking about Lawrence of Arabia, Rashida reminded me of the time we were living in the Middle East and of a road trip we made some 30 years ago when we took our young children to Madain Saleh, where we saw an archaeological site from the Nabatean kingdom not far from Madinah in northern Saudi Arabia. When the Nabateans flourished more than 2,000 years ago, Madain Saleh was the largest settlement of this civilisation after Petra in Jordan.

Elsewhere, tucked away in a corner of the desert, we saw evidence of Lawrence of Arabia's derring-do activities of 1917 from the First World War when he had blown up trains on the (now abandoned) Hijaz railway serving the Ottoman Empire, who were then overlords of Arabia.

I recall seeing some weather-beaten and well-rusted train carriages lying on their side in the soft, white sand next to a section of the track also still visible. Later, at another location nearby, we viewed a refurbished German locomotive which had seen service on this railway travelling between Damascus and Madinah.

Having paused to permit a bit of nostalgia, it was back to the present as we left Urfa by the Harran Gate. Murad pointed out to us that the city walls of Urfa, dating from the 9th century CE, had in part been quietly dismantled and picked at over the years with the 'borrowed' stonework used in the construction of houses by and for the local population. On closer inspection, the homes constructed with this historic material acquired from the impressive whiteish-yellow stone defensive ramparts were a dead give-away and easy to differentiate from other buildings. Urfa (formerly called Edessa) is itself an ancient urban settlement, having been continuously occupied for at least the past 11,000 years, i.e. from 9,000 BCE, and I say 'at least' as some archaeologists have hinted that it could even be older.

Question: how many different civilisations were in charge in Urfa before and after the Romans?

Answer: now, before I knew, I guessed three or four, at most six but when I researched this the number of civilisations that have at some stage in the past 'ruled' Urfa or played a significant role in the region is *at least* 12 (yes, you read that correctly, *at least 12*). Now, I was getting to understand better why Mesopotamia and its 'story' is such a richly textured, multi-layered one that has evolved over literally eons. Oh, and if you're interested, starting with the Neolithic (New Stone Age) there follows *at least* 12 subsequent civilisations: Hurrian, Hittite, Aramean, Assyrian, Achaemenid (Persian), Macedonian and Seleucid, Roman, Sassanid, Byzantine, Arab, Ottoman and, finally, the Turkish Republic.

That means (at least) a dozen different groups of people running the show in Urfa over the past 12,000 years or so and, in many cases, each one with their own belief system, set of laws, language, ways of writing and recording events, commercial dealings, architecture and art, social practices, military strategies, and so on.

Meanwhile, back in Northern Mesopotamia, we took just under an hour to drive the 45 km (28 miles) to Harran and our guide, not wishing to alarm us but equally desirous to 'put us in the picture' as it were geographically speaking, announced that we were now just 6 km (3.6 miles) from the border with Syria, but he did reassure us that we were safe.

Murad led us to an area of raised ground close to a wire fence that stretched for miles, in order to get a decent view of the surrounding area. It wasn't even 10am yet but the sun had already climbed high into the heavens in a cloudless sky and you just knew it was going to be a scorcher of a day, but we were well prepared for this with protective sun lotion, hats and lots of bottled water. Rashida had gone the extra mile by bringing an umbrella, which came in for good use. At one point, as we walked down a footpath to the site, our driver walked next to Rashida to avail of the protective shade of the brolly as even he found the sun too hot.

From our vantage point, we could see a tall, solitary tower standing with an arch nearby and there was a lot of building debris visible; these were the remains of the Grand Mosque of Harran. It occurred to me later that the tower of 50 m (164 ft) in height we had observed would have been the very same sight that Lawrence of Arabia would have referred to in his diary of just over a century previously, although on this occasion there was no mirage visible. Murad said that the scaffolding we could see was the evidence of continuing archaeological work on this site and elsewhere in Harran. The important thing to note about this Grand Mosque was that the broken pieces of stone, building remnants, *stelae* (Latin for ancient monuments) and other artefacts represent several structures that archaeologists believe formed part of different buildings – probably places of worship – from various eras including the Babylonian, Sabian, Roman, Christian, Islamic, etc.

This helps to explain the challenges archaeologists have when faced with a *mixum gatherum* collection of remains of the past scattered all over the place in a random chaotic manner, with no clear 'road signs' or 'markers' as to what each relic represents or from which year or period it dates from.

There is, of course, a contrary 'so what' theory of history when looking back over many thousands of years. On the one hand, it can be considered interesting but irrelevant or, on the other, a complete waste of effort being unconnected to how we live today in the 21st century. I would be the first to admit that strong arguments can be advanced to support this point of view. Throughout my life, however, I must admit, my quest has been to learn from the past, apply it to the present and the future, so as to render the future a better place for 'the happiness and liberty of millions yet unborn', (Joseph Warren oration, USA, 1775).

Just as a reminder that Harran goes back a long way, it is mentioned in the Old Testament of the Bible (Book of Genesis) where Terah, the father of Abraham, settled with his family in Harran before later journeying from there to Canaan.

> *And Terah took Abram his son, and Lot the son of Haran his son's son, and Sarai his daughter in law, his son Abram's wife; and they went forth with them from Ur of the Chaldees, to go to the land of Canaan; and they came unto Haran, and dwelt there.*
> Book of Genesis, Chapter 11, verse 31; as quoted from my father's King James Version of the Bible, dated 1932

> Please note: to avoid confusion, the first Haran touched on above is a person, the son of Terah and brother to Abram and Nahor. The second reference to Haran is the place itself in Mesopotamia: an alternative spelling of this location; also written in old texts as Charran.

As the quartet followed Murad, we noted that elsewhere around us in this area of Harran, there were farms and houses dotted around the flattish landscape. In the middle distance, amongst a clutch of trees and some thrown-together concrete dwellings, was a group of distinctive buildings with rounded roofs, as if from another era.

Historically, the earliest relics of religious worship found in the Harran area have been shown to be connected with *Sin*, the god of the moon and the chief of all gods.

The older fortified building next to some trees which had earlier caught my eye, was Harran Castle. This was constructed by the Romans as a stronghold to protect the city of 20,000 people on the site of the original Temple of Sin. The round-roofed domed houses were built according to an ancient design to facilitate ventilation to keep the inhabitants cool during the intense heat of summer.

At the site of the Temple of Sin, a team of Italian archaeologists in the 1970s unearthed a large collection of clay tablets in what was the ancient city of Ebla but what is now north-western Syria 80 km (50 miles) away from Antakya, which we had passed through two days previously. These ancient Ebla Tablets, written in two cuneiform 'alphabets', Sumerian and Eblaite, date back 4,500 years and are the first written records of Harran surviving to this day.

As we walked around the site of (the ruined) Harran Grand Mosque, also known as the Paradise Mosque, dating from the 8th century CE, we shared our thoughts on the ancient belief system that held Sin, the moon god, as its chief deity and how temples to this creed had been constructed. The core of the belief was that Sin, the god of the moon, was the focal point for worship, as that was where all life came from. The faithful of this ancient religion would gather at dawn, noon and sundown to pray, always facing north. A well-developed liturgy came into being and was recorded in their holy books.

Murad told us that between the 8th and 11th centuries CE in Harran, the Abbasid Muslim rulers permitted inhabitants of other faiths to carry on with their religion so long as they were 'people of the book', i.e. Christians, Jews, Sabians and Magians as being monotheistic and having 'revealed truth' at the core of the belief systems.

This story of shared spiritual space reminded me of an anecdote from a dear friend of ours, a former general in the Indian Army, who told us of an occurrence when he was posted as a young lieutenant to the Ladakh territory of northern India adjacent to the border with China. On setting up camp in this remote mountainous area, it was initially decided that the only roofed dwelling available was to be occupied by our friend's commanding officer. Realising his contingent of troops, however, were from four different faiths, Islam, Christianity, Hinduism and Sikhism, the most senior officer in charge decided instead to convert this simple unoccupied house into a place of communal worship where each of the four religions could occupy a single corner for purposes of prayer and devotion. This model of mutual spiritual respect proved to be a resounding success with all the soldiers of the same regiment being able to worship simultaneously without discord under the same roof.

I admit this anecdote speaks of an ideal situation where harmony can surmount religious difference, but unfortunately in parts of the world today it bears scant resemblance to reality.

Near the Grand Mosque and Harran Castle were the city walls and gates. Originally, there were seven gates possessing, in some cases, the names of the cities the roads led to: the East Gate of Baghdad, the West Gate of Aleppo, the North Gate of Anatolia, and also the Lion Gate, among others.

Murad suggested we move on to see the distinctive beehive-shaped dwellings we'd seen from afar and we began walking in that direction – the houses being about a half a mile distant.

Murad, Feray and Suat went on ahead while Rashida and I dawdled to look more at the landscape and take some photos. While doing this we came across a solitary camel and a hefty-looking cow with dark skin that shone in the sunlight. We then met up with a local woman accompanied by her three daughters. Although Arabic-speaking, the young girls were able to converse with a few words of English. Using a lot of sign language, we managed to chat with our new-found companions.

A little later, we rejoined our group arriving at the round-roofed houses. They are based on an ancient design dating back thousands of years where the inside of the building is fashioned so as to keep the family living inside cool in summer and warm in winter.

This conically shaped dwelling reminded me a little of the oast houses I'd seen in Kent in south-east England back in 1973 when as a teenager I'd worked on a hop farm near Faversham. Oast houses, with their characteristic towered architecture, are used for the drying out of the hops normally harvested in September for the brewing industry – different hops are grown to brew different types of beer. Hops look a bit like small clusters of barley and are possessed of a very strong odour which I'll never forget.

Sorry but I've diverted again – blame my restless grey matter. Meanwhile back in Harran, we were met by the local headman of the area – a distinguished-looking gentleman with a regal bearing, dressed like an Arabian prince. His flowing head dress, a *ghutra* – a piece of cotton cloth formed into a head scarf – is worn by men to protect them from the sun and sand. His *ghutra* was held in place by a gold-coloured *agal* – two strands of corded material, usually made from the hair of a goat and originally used by the Bedouin when living in the desert to bind the legs of their camels to stop them running off. Along with his light-blue coloured *thobe*, this headman cut a dapper figure in this arid landscape. I noticed that he conversed with our tour guide in fluent Turkish but with a pronounced Arabic accent.

The headman was interesting to talk to and obviously liked to swap stories with Murad. Though we asked permission, he did not allow any photos to be taken of him. Despite it being Ramadan, we were served Turkish tea under a tented awning more Arabic than Turkish and very reminiscent of Bedouin tents seen in the deserts of Arabia.

As we sat there sipping our tea, the conversation turned to a variety of topics concerning Harran – as jotted down in my notebook:

▷ Founded by Nemrut (Nimrod), of Mount Nemrut fame.

▷ Harran associated with several people mentioned in holy scripture, such as Moses, Rebekah, Lot and others.

▷ Tale of local Harran man suffering from a disability who wrote to Jesus Christ for help.

▷ According to holy scripture, the Garden of Eden where Adam and Eve dwelt may have been in the region of Mesopotamia. And talking about Eve reminds me of when Rashida and I would drive to work in Jeddah in the 1980s and we would regularly pass a local landmark known as Eve's Grave or Tomb on Kilo 4 of the Old Makkah Road where the biblical figure of Eve is reputedly interred.

▷ A builder of a place of worship in Harran who boasted that his temple was bigger than Aghia Sofia – a case, Murad said, of cultural and power-crazed one-upmanship.

▷ Early Christians lived in Harran when under the rule of the Roman Empire, and a holy well came to be used there.

▷ The Crusades came to Harran and took the same holy well to Constantinople (Istanbul) and put it in Aghia Sofia. After 1453, when Mehmet II took over Constantinople, Christians fleeing took the holy well with them and put it in the Vatican. Today you might say this well has clocked up a fair smattering of air miles over the centuries! This holy well is now apparently no longer in the Vatican but believed to be elsewhere in Italy at an unknown location. This latter anecdote reads a bit like a Dan Brown mystery tale.

▷ This region was very fertile in ancient times with three rivers, including the Jullab and Ballikh rivers, flowing through or near Harran. A traveller by the name of Eviachelevee (sic; my incorrect spelling of the renowned Ottoman explorer, Evliya Çelebi on hearing it originally, my cloth ears, don't you know) who long ago noted that when he journeyed from Harran to Bidar (sic): "no sun, all shade by trees", thus indicating the region was extremely well-served by these rivers and also very lush. These rivers have long since dried up. Further references to Evliya Çelebi are to be seen on Days 1, 3 and 8.

▷ A number of religious figures were associated with Harran, for example the prophet, Abraham and his grandson, Jacob; and monotheism is reputed to have come into existence or prominence in Harran, later replacing polytheism.

▷ It would appear, however, that there was a degree of overlap between the two forms of 'theisms'. For example, long after the Islamic Caliphate[15] was established in the 8th century, the Sabians were able to openly worship in Harran for more than half a millennium until the 13th century.

▷ Based on what Murad told us, I'd scrawled on my notebook during the course of Day 5/Monday 27th May 2019 and here it is verbatim; "Moses at Tektek mountain range on road to Harran goes to Damascus – met Iatro/ prophet Merdian People – Koran – Bible" (sic). I was mystified as to what this particular scribbled note referred to, let alone meant. What to do? So, I delved further into the subject of "Iatro Prophet Harran" and I was overawed when I came across a remarkable book, *How Modern Science Came Into The World* by H. Floris Cohen, published by the Amsterdam University Press in 2010. It was a 'lightbulb moment' for me as I read through this tome, as it touched on the intriguing historical trail of how ancient learning from the classical era came into modern Europe via the Islamic world more than a thousand years ago. I learnt that Harran had played a pivotal role in how valuable knowledge was passed on to future generations.

The [Islamic] realm not only encompassed large portions of the earlier Hellenist world and Persia but also Central Asia, bordered by both India and China. A commercial free zone extending from Cordoba to the Chinese border made wide and instructive traveling comparatively easy. Texts, no longer written on papyrus or parchment but on cheap paper, spread widely and were preserved all over the realm in libraries opened to the public for the first time in history. These developments in the possibilities of travel, preservation, and communication go some way toward explaining how the number zero and the decimal place system could be adopted from India, how the Taoist idea of achieving longevity through the elixir could reach the Islamic world, and how in mathematical astronomy not only Greek texts but also Persian and Indian ones were translated.

H. Floris Cohen, *How Modern Science Came Into The World*, Chapter II Greek nature-knowledge transplanted: the Islamic world, from translation to enrichment, pp. 95-96, 2010

This is what makes this subject matter so incredibly amazing as I read through the relevant references in H. Floris Cohen's book and come across a chap, a native of Harran, called Thabit ibn Qurra al-Harrani. He lived in the 9th century, practised the Sabian religion and was also a close friend of the Caliph. Our friend Thabit al-Harrani, in addition to speaking his native tongue, Syriac – related to Aramaic – was fluent in Greek, Latin and Arabic. Al-Harrani was also a prominent mathematician, scientist and astronomer, as well as possessing attributes as a translator. He translated a number of important classical works from the Greek (e.g. Pythagoras, Euclid, Ptolemy, Archimedes) into the other languages he spoke.

For instance, Nicolaus Copernicus, the Polish Renaissance mathematician and astronomer who lived from 1473–1543, quoted from (later Latin translations of) the work of Thabit al-Harrani and other learned sources from the Islamic world on planetary calculations. Al-Harrani, in turn, based his writings on the scientific efforts of Ptolemy some 1,800 years ago when attempting to compute accurately the length of the year on earth. These historical figures therefore – Ptolemy, al-Harrani and Copernicus – can be considered pre-cursors of modern science.

This amazing tale of knowledge shared and handed on, however, isn't confined to this star trio of learning and science. It stretches much further both backwards and forwards in time. The first of these notables in this illustrious trinity, Ptolemy was undoubtedly a genius and could have devised it all on his tod with a 'eureka' flash of inspiration. But drawing on the writing of H. Floris Cohen and the well-honed maxim that science is a community effort, however, my unrelenting curiosity prompted me to look a little deeper into who might have preceded Ptolemy and possibly influenced the Alexandrian-born polymath from the 2nd century CE. And lo, my inquisitive nature was mollified when I came across Hipparchus of Bithynia of the 2nd century BCE who Ptolemy acknowledges learning from and availing of the scientific findings of his predecessor. And then going even further back, who or what had inspired Hipparchus? Further research revealed the Babylonian Astronomical Diaries of the 7th century BCE had served as a useful source of reference for Hipparchus.

Don't worry, I'll leave it there as I don't want to overdo this historical review of how great ideas come about or are passed down through the ages, but it does bring to mind the following well-known quotation from Sir Isaac Newton, "If I have seen further it is by standing on the shoulders of Giants." It would appear this powerful "shoulders of giants" expression was first uttered by Bernard of Chartres in the 12th century CE.

My research has shown that a definite 'idea transmission pathway' exists and, in my own small way, I believe it can be drawn up for how modern science came into being with this simplified schema:

Babylonian Astronomical Diaries → Hipparchus of Bithynia → Ptolemy → Thabit ibn Qurra al-Harrani → Nicolaus Copernicus and Galileo Galilei → Isaac Newton → Albert Einstein et al.

Overleaf is a hand drawn sketch illustrating an idea transmission pathway stretching over a period of nearly 3,000 years.

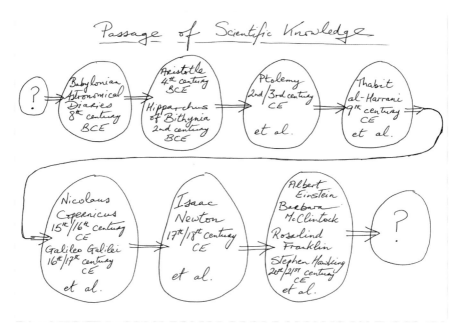

Sketch showing how scientific knowledge has been passed down over three millennia. Key figures noted above in this historical pathway played important roles at various stages in affecting how this valuable information was not just transmitted to future generations, but also refined or revised as new thinking and evidence came to light. An admirable thread of humility also parallels this transmission of wisdom as Hipparchus, Ptolemy, al-Harrani, Copernicus, Newton and Hawking acknowledged the achievements of those who preceded them in acquiring this precious learning.

Let those who are well-versed in such matters look deeper into this subject and go further back before the Babylonians or after Copernicus until the present day, while also amplifying the many stages in between. I'm always intrigued to learn how ideas get passed on.

This leads me on to mention something the science-fiction writer William Gibson has been quoted as saying: "The future is already here – it's just not evenly distributed" (*The Economist*, 4th December 2003). While Gibson's pithy turn of phrase underscores how the past, present and future are interrelated where advances in technology are concerned, his words also illustrate how the influence and distribution of such advances do not occur in a uniform or sequential manner. Instead, these developments are shaped by factors at play in society and show us that while technology and science possess enormous potential to transform people's lives for the better, the consequences may not always be beneficial or evenly distributed. Good governance should then work at ironing out any disparities in how technological innovations are experienced by all members of society.

But just before I leave Thabit ibn Qurra al-Harrani, let's consider why he was working as a translator in Harran. Under the leadership of the Abbasid Caliph, Caliph al-Mansur and his successors from the 8th century onwards, an age of openness to learning from other cultures was ushered in and then prospered as the Abbasids had control over or access to an enormous part of the globe stretching from Andalus in present-day Spain in the west and then to the east as far as China. When this came about, Thabit al-Harrani and others were able to congregate and work with a fairly free hand in translating all the important works from the classical Greek and Latin periods, including science, mathematics, history, literature and even travel writing. It was a 'golden age' of a kind and al-Harrani and fellow workers flourished in the city of Harran all those 1,300 years ago as the prevailing *mores* back then encouraged a genuine embrace of 'the other' in a positive and enlightened way. I would go as far as to suggest that Harrani and his contemporaries played a major contributory role in the development and transmission of knowledge at this key milestone of human evolution. Humanity has been the beneficiary, therefore, of this benevolent ethos.

To think I was in my 7th decade of life and I had never heard of Harran until this sojourn in Northern Mesopotamia, but having learnt a little bit more about this place, I feel as if I've discovered a box-full of treasures that has re-ignited my love of learning all over again.

With that we had reached our next location, the Urfa Archaeological Museum – another rabbit hole of stuff beckoned!

Our arrival in the early afternoon with the sun shining everywhere was on the dramatic side, as the site occupied by the museum is laid out to impress with its unashamed modernist architecture that has taken a leaf out of the minimal Bauhaus school of design but leavened with a gentle touch. The high, gently curving arches, subtly incorporating an Islamic theme, were set next to the main building itself, but I noted that when walking under the arches, that they not only provided welcome shaded relief from the strong sun now overhead but it also 'felt good' being in this place, as the tall structures conveyed in some understated way a sense of harmonious space and well-being. It's not often I can say that about modern architecture and hats off to the people who designed this memorable Urfa Archaeological Museum.

I'll be describing what we saw in the museum but two of the many exhibits are worth highlighting: the sculpture of Urfa Man (sometimes called Fish Lake Man) and the cuneiform script used in ancient Mesopotamia.

⌖ Urfa (Fish Lake) Man

Let's look at Urfa Man first: as Murad informed us as we walked into a section of the museum where what is reputed to be the oldest statue in the world, approximately

1.90 m (6 ft) in height and determined to be 11–12,000 years old, is on display. Urfa Man (ever so slightly larger than life size) is carved from sandstone and looks like a man standing with his arms at his sides and his hands held in front of his lower body; his legs are missing or perhaps they were never there in the first place. His eyes are jet black, made from the volcanic rock obsidian, and he is wearing a v-shaped necklace. The physiognomy of the head, arms and trunk of Urfa Man's body is realistic and yet, simultaneously, the minimalist approach to the carving of this sculpture gives it an eerie, other-worldly 'feel'.

This mysterious, uniquely detailed yet restrained form of statuary dates from the Upper Palaeolithic Age (i.e. the Upper Stone Age) which lasted for a lengthy period from 6,000 BCE going much further back by 42,000 years to 48,000 BCE. Urfa Man was excavated just 20 km (12 miles) distant from Urfa, at the archaeological site called Göbeklitepe.

⌗ Cuneiform

In addition to the Urfa Man exhibit at the museum, there is a complete section devoted to cuneiform. But what is cuneiform and what is its significance?

Let's first read the following:

Fate is a slippery bank that makes a man slide.
Whoever has walked with truth generates life.
Possessions are sparrows in flight which can find no place to alight.
The scribal art is the mother of orators and father of scholars.

Babylonian proverbs, dating back at least 5,000 years.

The Onset of the Deluge
The god Errakal was uprooting the mooring-poles,
Ninurta, passing by, made the weirs overflow.
The Annunaki gods carried torches of fire,
They lit up the land with their brightness.
The calm before the Storm-god came over the sky,
Everything light turned to darkness.

Myths from Mesopotamia, *The Epic of Gilgamesh*,
Old Babylonian version, circa 2,000 BCE
Tablet XI, ii, 101–106; Stephanie Dalley, Oxford University Press, 1989

The above-quoted Babylonian proverbs and extract from *The Epic of Gilgamesh* were first written in cuneiform script some 4–5,000 years ago and subsequently translated by scholars over the past 200 years to enable us today to understand this ancient culture and the story it has to tell.

Cuneiform is a form of writing on clay tablets, stone and metal but mostly on clay tablets, going back at least 5,500 years to when it was 'invented' in Mesopotamia where words, foodstuffs such as wheat and rice, finances, facts, ideas, philosophies, religious texts, housing deeds, guidance for children, food rations for workers, epic sagas and love poetry, literature, legal documents and peace treaties between warring nations – were all recorded for posterity in written format. Various cuneiform tablets have been unearthed from numerous sites over many years by archaeologists working in Mesopotamia.

But pause for a moment to think about this pivotal point in history. For eons and eons going back into prehistory, people passed on knowledge, information and even 'breaking news' by word of mouth. All data was held in a human version of RAM (Random Access Memory) where details necessary for life were kept in people's heads. Nothing was written down. Memory was the key here, with illiteracy the norm.

Then, somebody somewhere in Mesopotamia circa 3,500 BCE came up with the idea of writing stuff down and it was in the form of mini pictures that encapsulated the idea, the activity or the item being talked about and thus a 'pictographic' way of writing was born, i.e. a pictorial representation of what was under discussion came into existence through the inventive creativity of someone. Writing was born. Other examples of pictographic forms of writing are ancient Egyptian hieroglyphics, and modern Chinese and Japanese. In Mesopotamian cuneiform, these mini pictures or pictographs were primitive at first and underwent modification over many years to become simpler and less like the appearance of the original thing being written about; it also made it easier and therefore quicker to write.

Cuneiform actually means 'wedge-shaped' (from the Latin, *cuneus*: wedge-shaped) and is so named because the very first scribes devised a means of using a wedge-shaped stylus fashioned from the reeds that were growing in abundance by the rivers Euphrates and Tigris which could be pressed into damp clay, also freely available by the banks of the same two rivers and then availing of 600–1,000 characters to produce words. The clay was given sufficient time to dry and become a hardened solid tablet. Depending on the importance of the written material and its context, such tablets (e.g. a shopping list) could be very small and could fit in the palm of your hand or could be something of great national importance, such as an official peace treaty or the Sumerian King List (i.e. a comprehensive list of rulers of Mesopotamia from pre-history up to the then present which would have been 4,000 years ago, written in the Sumerian language using cuneiform script) and therefore larger in size.

There were many examples of cuneiform on display at the Urfa Archaeological Museum and it is fascinating to note that this form of writing lasted for about 3,000 years until the 1st century CE when it became extinct. Then, in the 18th and 19th centuries, various learned souls beavering away on cuneiform in Germany, France Britain and Ireland worked at – or perhaps I should say laboured at – deciphering this way of extinct writing. How to go about it? Working on a principle of using and comparing coincidental linguistic texts obtained from one place, such as the Rosetta Stone (involving the use of juxtaposed known and unknown text) which was acquired by, ahem, the British (by military conquest from the French in 1802 in Egypt) and was found to have three different languages inscribed on this greyish piece of damaged granodiorite rock – a bit like granite – which were: Egyptian Hieroglyphics, Demotic or Cursive Coptic (a descendant of Ancient Egyptian) and (classical) Greek and dates from 196 BCE. But I'm going to be pedantic here, because of course, geologically speaking, the Rosetta Stone is millions of years old and by the way is from the Aswan area of Egypt.

But the point here is that while the Egyptian hieroglyphics were the unknown quantity, the Demotic and Greek scripts were already understood and could be used to help 'translate' the meaning of the hieroglyphs. Over the next 20 years or so in the early 19th century, scholars were able to decode the Rosetta Stone and the mysteries of the Egyptian hieroglyphics were resolved.

But with cuneiform there was a huge problem, as there was no equivalent of the Rosetta Stone that could help in this translation/deciphering process until, by amazing happenstance, in 1835, Sir Henry Rawlinson, a British chap who was in Persia (present-day Iran) went to see an archaeological place of interest well known for centuries but little understood. It was the Behistun Inscription which is located near the present-day city of Kermanshah in western Iran. On a rock face is carved an important regal inscription by King Darius of Persia dating from 2,500 BCE and it is written in three languages: Babylonian, Elamite and Old Persian.

Since Old Persian was a known quantity, it was used as a 'linguistic bridgehead' to translate the other two languages, and three experts in the field of cuneiform at the time – Sir Henry Rawlinson (British), Julius Oppert (French/German) and the Reverend Edward Hincks (Irish), who were known as the 'holy trinity of cuneiform' – worked at making the Babylonian cuneiform intelligible during the 19th century.

After working on it for a while, the three men came up with a translation of the Behistun Inscription and it proved to be a historical monologue from King Darius of Persia with the opening phrase: "I am Darius, the great king, king of kings, the king of Persia, the king of countries, the son of Hystaspes, the grandson of Arsames, the Achaemenid … etc." extolling his virtues as a ruler, detailing his victories in battle and also yielding a very useful family tree for King Darius and other members of the Achaemenid dynasty.

Thanks to the determined efforts of Rawlinson, Oppert, Hincks and others, the above cuneiform writing and many thousands of other Mesopotamian clay tablets have been translated for the world to understand the recorded details of the Sumerian, Babylonian, Assyrian and other cultures of antiquity that had lain silent for thousands of years.

Another really important aspect of cuneiform to bear in mind is that at first it was used as a handy accounting and recording tool to keep a check on goods, foodstuffs, animals and money – things that were easily quantifiable and vital for day-to-day living. This really was how cuneiform was used initially and then, many years later, someone came up with the game-changing notion that cuneiform could be used to record what people said. This was revolutionary. Cuneiform was then modified and developed to write down phonetically what people actually said so that it became, among other things, syllabic in how it was written down. As a result, cuneiform made a giant leap from being a pictographic script to becoming more complex at recording not only what people said, but nuanced language could now be documented also on these many clay tablets so that poetry, literature, humour, ideas, philosophy and other abstract thinking could be retained for posterity. Also, cuneiform was initially written right to left and the scribes would mark out designated lines where the text would be impressed into the soft, damp clay.

Personally, I'm tickled that an Irishman, the previously mentioned Reverend Hincks, a clergyman educated at Trinity College Dublin no less, a noted Assyriologist in his day, made notable contributions to the decipherment of cuneiform in his spare time when not fulfilling his duties as a rector in a country parish in Killyleagh, Co. Down, Northern Ireland.

The Urfa Archaeological Museum is to be congratulated for having such a splendid display of this cultural phenomenon of recording history from so long ago.

We departed from the museum and Murad proposed the Urfa Haleplibahce (in Turkish this means Aleppo garden) Mosaic Museum which, we were informed, is dedicated to the Amazons. Luckily this second museum was within easy walking distance, about half a kilometre away. As we strolled through the well-laid out garden setting that thankfully adjoined these two museums, Murad drew something of interest to our attention: the Kizilkoyun (in Turkish this means red sheep) Necropolis. On our left was a hill of bare rock stretching for several hundred metres in either direction with contemporary houses perched on top. This necropolis (which originates from the classical Greek meaning city of the dead) had been wrought from the rock sometime between the years 100–400 CE and recent archaeological excavation work had uncovered bodies entombed there and also some remarkable floor mosaics. This necropolis had been used by people to live in for hundreds of years and, until relatively recently, a shanty town had existed within the many caves dotted around the hillside.

After a short walk, we arrived at the Urfa Mosaic Museum and couldn't miss the eye-catching futuristic architecture which gave the building the appearance of an impressive spaceship at rest. The focal point of the display was a largescale artwork depicting the Amazons on horseback in combat against their enemy and in one of the illustrations, fighting against some lions. What is interesting about these fêted warriors of old is that they were all women and they were used as mercenary soldiers by the Romans. According to legend, the Amazons were from the Thermodon River in what is now near the town of Terme in central Türkiye. This waterway exists to this day as the Terme River flowing into the Black Sea.

While gazing at this display of Amazonian prowess on the battlefield, we also viewed the many beautiful mosaics on show. It was then that Murad told us about the Sumerian Tablets – supposedly the Flood Tablets – a collection of ancient artefacts detailing the well-known story of the flood that covered the earth in antiquity. The Flood. Where to begin? The Flood (or Deluge) is recorded in the holy writings of various religions: the Bible (Christianity), the Qur'an (Islam), the Tanakh (Judaism), the Satapata Brahmana and the Puranas (Hinduism) and the Kitab-i-Aqdas (Baha'i faith).

If we examine a period much earlier than our own, the Babylonian era, archaeologists have uncovered clay tablets (in the Sumerian language, written in cuneiform) dating as far back as 2,100 BCE, i.e. up to 4,100 years ago, which mention *The Epic of Gilgamesh* for the first time. Then at varying periods subsequently, up to 600 BCE (i.e. 2,600 years ago) the written record also in cuneiform but on that subsequent occasion representing the Akkadian language (which by now had become the *lingua franca* of Mesopotamia), differing versions of this epic were produced, which was a work of creative endeavour on a mammoth scale and, to date, *The Epic of Gilgamesh* is the oldest example of literature that has come down to us.

This heroic tale is about 76,000 words long, the average length of a novel. It is not religious scripture but it does encompass a huge spectrum of tales filled with gods, kings and diverse divine or human characters, tales of derring-do, slaughter, cruelty, and the story of the Great Flood, but also love, sex – the full-frontal kind – friendship, self-doubt, realisation of mortality, and so much more which includes some of the following: the meeting of and deep friendship of two main protagonists, Gilgamesh, a king and Enkidu, a wild man later 'tamed'; the tale of the Cedar Forest and the slaying of Humbaba, the King of the Cedar Forest; the Tale of Ishtar, a goddess who is also a prostitute; the Bull of Heaven; the death of Enkidu as prescribed by the gods; the Great Flood.

Then, Siduri, goddess of wine and beer, spoke some home truths to the headstrong and narcissistic Gilgamesh advising him to live life as follows:

Gilgamesh, where do you roam?
You will not find the eternal life you seek.
When the gods created humankind
The appointed death for humankind,
Kept eternal life in their own hands.
So, Gilgamesh, let your stomach be full,
Day and night enjoy yourself in every way,
Every day arrange for pleasures.
Day and night, dance and play,
Wear fresh clothes.
Keep your head washed, bathe in water,
Appreciate the child who holds your hand,
Let your wife enjoy herself in your lap.
This is the lot of humankind.

Myths from Mesopotamia, *The Epic of Gilgamesh,*
Old Babylonian version, circa 2,000 BCE
Tablet X, iii, 1-14; Stephanie Dalley, Oxford University Press, 1989

According to some Assyriologists and biblical scholars, the above extract of 14 lines from *The Epic of Gilgamesh* acted as the forerunner for similar counsel as laid down in Ecclesiastes in the Old Testament of the Bible and further studies have indicated that this ancient epic could have served as base material for sacred writings in other religions. As stated previously, this poem is not regarded as religious but the jury is still out on the influence it has exerted on other texts, some sacred, some literary and experts from various quarters continue to carry out research into ancient documents to see if they serve their arguments. I don't see this matter being resolved anytime soon though.

By the way, we owe a great debt of gratitude to the Assyriologist George Smith (1840–76) who started out in life from humble origins. On leaving school at 14, George became an engraver for a London firm producing legal tender bank notes. In his free time and his lunch hour, he would visit the British Museum and study the Sumerian, Assyrian and Babylonian artefacts on show, including the cuneiform tablets. George Smith taught himself cuneiform and went on to become an employee at the British Museum, serving as an assistant to Sir Henry Rawlinson (translator of Behistun Inscription mentioned previously).

The story is told of George Smith that one day while at the British Museum during one of his lunch breaks, he was looking at one of the 12 clay cuneiform tablets containing *The Epic of Gilgamesh* which, up to then, nobody had been able to understand since ancient times. As he attempted to decipher the wedge-shaped characters, he suddenly realised he could understand what he was reading. It was a 'eureka' moment for George and he is said to have shouted out his delight and then proceeded to run around the Reading Room of the British Museum. Later, George Smith wrote that it was thrilling to have been the first person in 2,000 years to be able to read and understand *The Epic of Gilgamesh*.

Another Assyriologist of note is Hormuzd Rassam (born 1826 in Mosul, present-day Iraq) who is known for contributing to the translation of the clay tablets of *The Epic of Gilgamesh*. He is believed to be the first Middle Eastern Assyrian archaeologist from the Ottoman Empire. By the way, Mr Rassam emigrated to England and resided in Brighton, becoming a British citizen. He subsequently assisted the government to help free British diplomats from captivity in Ethiopia.

Bear with me as I stay with *The Epic of Gilgamesh* as I believe this poem possesses immense value even for us today in our contemporary world. I'm ashamed to admit that I read this incredible piece of literature from antiquity for the first time at the age of 65, but when I did, I was spellbound by it.

Like a Shakespearean play with its recognisable (and reassuring) construct with the ever-present iambic meter which acts as a sustaining cadence throughout the drama, *The Epic of Gilgamesh* too has its recurring rhythmical form – a very simple structure based on a line or two lines making up a sentence with just one or two things, ideas or events mentioned. No rhyming. And yet, this poem is an epic in every sense of the word as it not only tells an amazing set of stories (as I've previously touched on) but it also transcends so many aspects of our existence as human beings such as life and death, love and friendship, justice, and searching for meaning.

Here are some examples which I'll leave you to ponder on:

Tablet X, lines 301–307
The Wisdom of Utanapishti: Death
Man is snapped off like a reed in a reed bed!
The comely young man, the pretty young woman –
All too soon in their prime Death abducts them!

No one at all sees Death,
no one at all sees the face of Death,
no one at all hears the voice of Death,
Death so savage, who hacks men down.

Tablet X, lines 308–315
The Wisdom of Utanapishti: The Mayfly
Ever do we build our households,

ever do we make our nests,
ever do brothers divide their inheritance,
ever do feuds arise in the land.

Ever the river that has risen brings us the flood,
the mayfly floating on the water.
Their faces look upon the face of the sun,
then all of a sudden nothing is there!

What is enchanting about *The Epic of Gilgamesh* is that it begins and ends with a disarmingly simple yet profound message while circumscribing an enormous arc of experience lived through by the hero, Gilgamesh:

The Prologue
Tablet I, lines 18–18
Climb Uruk's* wall and walk back and forth!
Survey its foundations, examine the brickwork!
Were its bricks not fired in an oven?
Did the Seven Sages not lay its foundations?

A square mile is city, a square mile date-grove, a square mile is claypit, half a
square mile the temple of Ishtar: three square miles and a half is Uruk's expanse.
See the tablet box of cedar,
release its clasps of bronze!
Lift the lid of its secret,
pick up the tablet of lapis lazuli and read out –
The travails of Gilgamesh, all that he went through.

Tablet XI, Lines 323–328
Conclusion
The epic ends as it began;
O Ur-shanabi*, climb Uruk's wall and walk back and forth!
Survey its foundations, examine the brickwork!
Were its bricks not fired in an oven?
Did the Seven Sages not lay its foundations?

A square mile is city, a square mile date-grove, a square mile is claypit, half a
square mile the temple of Ishtar: three square miles and a half is Uruk's expanse.

The full circle of life, you could say.

My own understanding of this legend is that allowing for the allegorical element in the poem, it can be seen that "Uruk's expanse" represents the sum of human life; that the "city" stands for the places where we live and how each successive generation replaces the previous one; the "date-grove" can be thought of as the food which must be produced and consumed throughout one's life; the "claypit" means the working life that must be entered into and finally the "temple" can illustrate the spiritual and intellectual life lived by us all.

Like all good stories, there is a symmetry to the entire poem with the original imagery and ideas mentioned at the start repeated again at the very end, and note how at the beginning it mentions the "travails" of Gilgamesh – this was not just a straightforward adventure – there was pain involved and our hero has learnt some valuable lessons through his 'journey' in his lengthy search for meaning.

While writing this (in May 2020) during the Covid Pandemic, some 'breaking news' appeared:[16, 17]

U.S. federal prosecutors are seeking the return to Iraq of a roughly 3,500-year-old clay tablet purchased by the Hobby Lobby arts and crafts store chain for display in the Washington, D.C.-based Museum of the Bible. The cuneiform tablet is described as "stolen Iraqi property" in a civil complaint filed Monday.

The complaint details part of the journey of this fragment of the oldest known creation tale — from a palace library in ancient Mesopotamia to its present location in a Department of Homeland Security warehouse in Queens, New York.

It alleges that a major international auction house, unnamed in the complaint, obscured the provenance of the tablet, known as the Gilgamesh Dream Tablet, when it sold the tablet to Hobby Lobby in 2014.

Agents from U.S. Immigration and Customs Enforcement's Homeland Security Investigations seized the tablet last year from the Museum of the Bible, which, it said, cooperated with the investigation. Hobby Lobby's owners are the founders of the Museum of the Bible.

The prosecutors said the 5-by-6-inch tablet, which Hobby Lobby purchased for more than $1.6 million, is considered the property of the Iraqi government and should be returned.

"Whenever looted cultural property is found in this country, the United States government will do all it can to preserve heritage by returning such artefacts where they belong," Richard Donoghue, U.S. attorney for the Eastern District of New York, said in a statement.

The Gilgamesh epic is a Sumerian poem believed to have been written at least 4,000 years ago. Sections of it mirror details of the Great Flood and the

Garden of Eden stories from the Old Testament, which it predates.
A 12-tablet version of the poem, written in the Akkadian language, was discovered in the ruins of a library in the palace of Nineveh in present-day Mosul, Iraq.

Author's note: it was subsequently handed over to the Iraqi government and in early December 2021, the Gilgamesh Dream Tablet was unveiled in Baghdad by Iraqi foreign minister, Fuad Hussein and the nation's culture minister, Hassan Nazim.

The Gilgamesh Dream Tablet

On exiting the Urfa Mosaic Museum, Murad suggested a hotel nearby (Hotel El Ruha) which boasts of having a grotto in the basement. Off we trooped and after a short walk where we passed Urfa Castle high up on a hill and near to, we were informed, the birthplace of Abraham (Ibrahim, the prophet). We arrived at said hostelry where we were warmly greeted and shown to the subterranean cavern. Pictures were duly taken to record the event.

Murad then announced that we needed to get a move on if we wanted to see Göbeklitepe, next on our 'to-do list'. But first things first as Suat stated, on more than one occasion, "This trip, Nicholas, is not just about 'old stuff' as much as we like it but we also need to see to our tummies from time to time!" The ever so subtle hint was taken and we stopped at a local Urfa *han*, or inn. A fine lunch was had, some refreshing beverages supped, and all was well with the quartet.

Göbeklitepe

We drove the 20 km (12 miles) to Göbeklitepe on near empty roads and en route Murad reminded us that it was located in the northern part of the Fertile Crescent within the cradle of civilisation. Although discovered in 1963, this archaeological site has only recently come into prominence thanks to the sterling work of the late Klaus Schmidt, a German archaeologist. Over a 20-year period from 1994 until his untimely death in 2014, Schmidt devoted his tremendous energies to uncovering – both physically and historically – the story that is Göbeklitepe. According to Schmidt, this archaeological site is "the first human-built holy place". By the way, Göbeklitepe translates into English as 'pot-bellied hill'.

On our arrival at this rural setting where farms and fields aplenty are to be seen interspersed with flattish areas and rolling hills, we approached the site on foot along a wooden walkway leading from the car park. It is interesting to note that only 5 per cent of this site has been excavated archaeologically and it is estimated many other amazing finds await discovery under the Turkish earth. This has become known thanks to ground-penetrating radar which has been used to peep into what still lies hidden underground.

As we got closer, I noted the sweeping curved lines of the enclosure covering the excavated portion of Göbeklitepe and, like the Urfa Mosaic Museum, this ancient site was on a grand scale architecturally with the roof shaped a bit like a flying saucer. Here we were in the middle of the countryside about to enter a special place with a connection to the very distant past. The wooden path led onto an elevated platform surrounding the archaeological site and it was ingeniously positioned so that visitors could look down on the ancient remains from a raised vantage point. Thoughtfully, a roof had been added and this acted as a shelter against the elements, thus protecting not only people present but also the limestone megaliths, pillars and stone structures arranged in what appeared to be a number of concentric circles.

Some of the pillars had carvings of animals such as a lizard, a boar, an auroch (an ancient large bull now extinct), a fox, a gazelle and a donkey. Birds were represented with the recognisable form of a crane and a vulture visible. In addition, snakes and other reptiles were shown; also, there was a lionlike figure along with some insects and arachnids.

Why was limestone selected for the construction of this complex? Two possible reasons:

▷ As this rock was in plentiful supply locally, it made perfect sense to avail of this easily available building material.

▷ There is archaeological evidence from Northern Mesopotamia and other ancient sites around the world to suggest that peoples of long ago selected a certain kind of rock for the construction of places of worship, for instance, based on the inherent spiritual qualities of that rock and its connection to the deity. It is conceivable, therefore, that the local limestone was deemed to possess these necessary divine merits.

As we stood there looking down, we were in awe of what we saw: Göbeklitepe is believed to be the oldest human-built religious site in the world at between 11–12,000 years old. It predates the Egyptian pyramids by 6,500 years, Stonehenge in the UK by 6–7,000 years and Knowth and Newgrange in Ireland by 6,000 years.

According to Schmidt, Göbeklitepe is within the 'Golden Triangle' area in the uppermost part of the Fertile Crescent and this was where some very important things were happening once the last Ice Age had come to an end in 13,000 BCE, i.e. 15,000 years ago. The way of life observed by the population of Mesopotamia began to change dramatically. Up to then, communities of nomadic hunter gatherers dispersed around the region, migrated from place to place subsisting on what was available for food and shelter in an area and moving on to 'greener pastures' once the bounty of a locality had been consumed. But this social norm came to be transformed when people began to adopt a more sedentary existence with the simultaneous development of agriculture and the domestication of animals.

Murad informed us that exciting evidence of this intersection between two very different livelihoods had been discovered in the local area, as surviving specimens of ancient wild wheat – such as einkorn and emmer – were found in the vicinity, as well as samples of domesticated wheat.

In addition, the archaeological artefacts unearthed in Göbeklitepe and as interpreted by Schmidt have given rise to vigorous discussions along the lines of a 'chicken and egg scenario': which came first, religion or agriculture?

Meanwhile, these substantial changes to human existence in the Neolithic Period (New Stone Age) were occurring for a number of reasons: the prevailing climate was suitable for human habitation; the Mesopotamian Plain is relatively flat; the area is well-served by rivers of which the Tigris and the Euphrates play a major role; the land is naturally fertile and served as a useful food source. Evidence points to this Golden Triangle with the upper apex of the triangle in what is now south-eastern Türkiye, a little to the west of Lake Van, the western pointy bit being in what is now northern Lebanon and the eastern point of this three-sided epicentre of advancing civilisation was in present-day northern Iraq just to the east of the River Tigris.

You could say this triangle of territory played a unique role in advancing civilisation in both the physical and philosophical senses. A unique version of serendipity was operating in this space where a host of factors – geological, geographical, meteorological, agricultural, social, spiritual and philosophical – somehow coalesced in the 'right' way at the 'right' time and in the 'right' place which enabled this group of people to take tentative steps towards charting a new pathway to a 'better place', to finding a more civilised *modus vivendi*.

Isn't that what we're still doing all these years later? Aren't we always in search of a better life?

Schmidt went on to say that the ancient people living up to 12,000 years ago who constructed this site devoted to sacred worship also possessed an understanding of astronomy, as certain tall pillars which are 'T-shaped' were incorporated into the structure of Göbeklitepe and placed, as Schmidt maintained, in alignment with stars in the sky as they were thousands of years ago.

This connectivity of something holy on earth to the distant cosmos is also to be seen in the Egyptian pyramids, Stonehenge and Newgrange. The physical alignment of ancient religious structures with the heavens can also be seen in other parts of the world, such as Teothuacán in Mexico and Nabta Playa in the Nubian Desert of Egypt.

Prehistoric precision engineering where astronomy is concerned reminds me of when I was at Newgrange in Ireland in the early 1990s with my family. Now, the story is told that way back in 1699 when digging a grassy mound in a field in the Boyne Valley, County Meath, a landowner made a remarkable discovery. By chance, the entrance to what later became known as Newgrange Passage Tomb had been unearthed, one of the largest of its kind in western Europe and dating back to 3,200 BCE.

Newgrange Passage Tomb

Thirty years ago on that family visit, I remember well how our young but extremely well-informed guide took us through the Passage Tomb, pointing out significant details such as the knowledge required in prehistory to construct such a megalithic monument, the different stones (some decorated with elaborate designs) used for the passageway, the walls and also the corbelled roof arrangement. But the most dramatic part of Newgrange must be the placement of the stones over the main door to the Passage Tomb so as to create a strategic gap which acts as a lightbox on the winter solstice, usually 21st December, when sunlight shines through for 17 minutes shortly after sunrise on the shortest day of the year and the light travels the entire length of the passageway, illuminating the interior chamber.

I recall how my young son, Oliver and nephew, S. stood in front of our guide lapping up every word he uttered and then plyed him with numerous questions, so mesmerised were they with the magic of the moment. The adults too were no less amazed. Also present on that memorable day were my younger son, Justin and niece, K.

Interestingly, the Irish for winter solstice is 'grianstad an gheimhridh' (pronounced 'greeanstod un geerig') and the actual Irish word for solstice is 'grianstad' which translates as the stopping of the sun – 'grian' (sun) and 'stad' (stop). When I pause to think about it, there was a certain Celtic logic at work here as the days stopped getting shorter at the winter solstice, which served as a trustworthy celestial brake every year where earthly seasons were concerned and from the following day, the days began increasing in length very gradually until the summer solstice.

For the record, solstice itself derives from the Latin: 'sol' meaning sun and 'sistere', to stand still.

Now, in addition to the examples of Newgrange and Knowth I've described, there's also the important archaeological site of Carrowkeel in Co. Sligo in the north-west of Ireland.[18] It's a megalithic passage tomb complex dating back to the Neolithic Era – 4th millennium BCE. At this point let me quote from an eminent Irish naturalist, explorer and writer, Robert Lloyd-Prager, who penned the following about the discovery of Carrowkeel: "I had the privilege of being first to crawl down the entrance-passage and did so with no little awe. I lit three candles and stood awhile, to let my eyes accustom themselves to the dim light. There was everything just as the Bronze Age man had left it, three to four thousand years before. A light brownish dust covered all" (Praeger, 1937).

Imagine the excitement Praeger and colleagues would have felt when first unearthing these tombs back in 1911. Subsequent fieldwork and studies have yielded an array of fascinating details of this Neolithic Age settlement, including DNA evidence from the remains of six individuals pointing to ancestral origins in Anatolia – i.e. present-day Türkiye. In a way, this further demonstrates how links between the north-west of Europe (in the form of contemporary Ireland) and the eastern edge of the same continent (Türkiye of today) have existed for millennia.

Carrowkeel is a grouping of 26 passage tombs on high ground in the south of Co. Sligo located on the Bricklieve Hills that look out over Lough Arrow. Interestingly, there is a link with Irish mythology as Carrowkeel forms part of the legendary Moytura where the ancient celtic deities in the form of the *Tuatha De Danann* and the *Femorians* battled it out in that part of Ireland.

When I reflect on those undergrad field trips of mine back of 50 years ago I've referred to previously, I thank my lucky stars I had the opportunity to be able to experience the practical side of what I was getting to grips with in the natural sciences. These excursions led by the academic staff in the disciplines of geography and geology in all weathers to all four corners of the country and one memorable expedition abroad to Yorkshire complemented the abstract learning process. This was the exciting hands-on counterpoint of increasing one's knowledge of the great age of fossils or various rock specimens or how the tectonic plates ruled the Earth's surface, or finding out how an oxbow lake was formed or why an urban centre thrived or declined in the Middle Ages. It was heady stuff for a young'un such as myself as I was so hungry for knowledge of my chosen subject, the natural sciences. I was impatient to see how 'all this shit fits together' and, in a way, this has been an abiding mantra of mine throughout my life.

Entrance to one of the megalithic passage tombs, Carrowkeel, Co. Sligo, Ireland – dating back to the 4th millennium BCE.

Fast forward to 2019 and Feray, Suat, Rashida and I felt a similar childlike enchantment when spending those valuable moments in Göbeklitepe: feasting our eyes on a megalithic monument some 12,000 years old that was in commune with its nearby surroundings of Northern Mesopotamia and also the distant cosmos.

Schmidt maintained that this site had been erected by a people whose name we don't know, whose language we are ignorant of and that it came about 6,000 years before the existence of writing. He went on to say that Göbeklitepe was built exclusively for spiritual and ritual purposes only with, as he saw it, no evidence of people having lived there. More recent work onsite, however, has prompted other archaeologists to express reservations about this view, advancing a counter theory that perhaps people in antiquity did live in Göbeklitepe. The current re-examination of this iconic site has led to controversy, as some of the latest thinking is sceptical of Göbeklitepe's celestial links.

One other salient point to bear in mind about this special place was that writing, even cuneiform, hadn't yet been invented as thousands of years still had to pass before these wedge-shaped characters impressed on wet clay came into regular use. The depiction of the various creatures on the megaliths, however, is thought to be a precursor of writing and perhaps served a symbolic or spiritual function known to the population of the region of 12 millennia ago. Sadly, when these people died out, their collective 'RAM' died with them, as nothing was recorded about their way of life, their culture, their language and so on.

Murad told us he had known the archaeologist Klaus Schmidt, who sadly died in 2014 at the age of 60, and the German archaeologist is still remembered with great fondness by local people as he put this Mesopotamian landmark 'on the map' as it were. The local people were very grateful for this recognition.

Schmidt's ground-breaking work (please excuse the pun) has nevertheless helped us gain an insight into the prehistoric people who constructed Göbeklitepe. It is hoped that further research in years to come will throw more light on that long-past civilisation.

By the way, we were chuffed that coincidental with the year of our visit, it turns out that 2019 was the 'Year of Göbeklitepe'. Since then, I have carried out a lot of research into this topic and I started writing this book during the Covid Pandemic lockdown period of 2020–21.

In May 2021, it was announced the Turkish government was proposing that a replica of a Göbeklitepe 5.5 m (18 ft) stele* was to be displayed at the United Nations Headquarters in New York, USA.

(Update – July 2022: It was reported in September 2021 that Türkiye gave a replica of a Göbeklitepe stele to be on public display at the UN headquarters in New York, USA.)

Göbeklitepe will come to be seen as a significant game changer, I believe, in how we comprehend the route of civilisation taken throughout history. But what do I understand by the all-encompassing term, civilisation? It can be likened to an artery of societal development that has flowed through the millennia of human existence being fed by many tributaries with mixed results while embracing numerous extremes: both positive, including enlightenment, progress and civility, but also negative, with dogmatism, regression and cruelty being part of the 'picture', and of course everything else in between. The mysteries being uncovered at Göbeklitepe will now enable this flawed highway that civilisation has trodden on to be traced even further back to 12,000 years ago and perhaps beyond.

An intriguing aspect to all this, however, which Schmidt hinted at, was that the site of Göbeklitepe can be viewed as the apex of societal development by the group of people who constructed this ancient place of worship. If that is the case, then it is conceivable that this prehistoric community can date its existence even further back than the calculated timeline of 12,000 years. A tantalising prospect, as it tempts one to think that civilisation can trace its roots well into the Mesolithic Era (Middle Stone Age) which goes back 20,000 years. All this does prompt another pathway of inquiry regarding the length of time people (i.e. *Homo sapiens* to give us our official scientific name, and by the way, this type of Latinised nomenclature is all down to an 18th-century Swede, Carl Linnaeus who developed a holistic methodology to categorise all living things on earth and is known as the 'father of taxonomy') have existed on this planet and the imprint left behind for future generations to discover, ponder on and try to explain.

Let's consider us human beings in this (extended timeline) context and as we proceed, please excuse the following jawbreaker, paleoanthropologists – experts on the study of human evolution, drawing on knowledge and expertise from the fields of science, biology, geology, geography, archaeology and, of course, anthropology – have estimated that people like us today have been around for about 300,000 years. But the story doesn't end there.

Our human evolutionary history has origins in the distant past where other human-like species have existed, such as *Neanderthal, Australopithecus* and *Homo erectus* just to name a few. Let's select *Australopithecus*, considered to be the oldest hominid who first walked this earth as far back as 4,200,000 (or, if you prefer, 4.2 million) years ago. I can hear you say, what's the point of all this? I'm coming to it, honest: people, in one form or another, have existed on this planet for millions of years and yet, we can only unearth proof of past civilisations that are thousands or just over 10,000 years old. Just because there is absence of evidence from way beyond millennia to several mega-annums (Ma, millions of years) ago does not denote evidence of absence. But the proverbial elephant in the room surely is, if people have been on this planet for up to 4.2 Ma, then where are the remnants, the broken jugs, the ruins of old settlements, the tools, the ancient detritus of past civilisations, thus being the evidence of developed societies which may have existed for lengthy periods as long-gone humanoid subsets?

Just imagine if archaeologists were to dig up some age-old site where it could be proved that human civilisation was older than 300,000 years. Wouldn't that discovery challenge a multitude of long-cherished ideas and beliefs about the origins of humanity? Also, wouldn't that trigger a re-evaluation of our understanding of how civilisations came about? A radical rethink would then be on the existential horizon.[19, 20]

There are a number of good books on Göbeklitepe, but if you had to read just one, may I suggest *Göbekli Tepe Genesis of the Gods: The Temple of the Watchers and the Discovery of Eden*, by Andrew Collins and Graham Hancock.

This is one exploration of the subject matter which is very much of the 'thinking outside the box' variety.

Let's take another moment to reflect a little further on our journey so far. Think about those far-off, ancient days when a group of people, who conceived and created Göbeklitepe, came into being, flourished for a time and faded away. They in turn were followed by the Akkadians, Sumerians, Hittites, Babylonians and many others who held sway in the Fertile Crescent and they all faded away. Later, they were followed by Alexander the Great and he faded away; then the Romans reigned supreme for a while and they too faded away. The Sassanians and others were in the ascendant for a time and they faded away, and right now, the 21st century is upon us.

If I pivot my attention 180 degrees and attempt to look ahead, I wonder what future generations will make of us as people with what might remain of our *modus vivendi* such as buildings, technology, mobile phones, social media, modes of transport, places of worship, pictures, weapons and other stuff.

When you consider Göbeklitepe and its position in the incredible sequence of human cultural development played out over enormous spans of time in straightforward human terms like this, it does become mind-bending.

It also serves to remind us how short a spell we have on this earth:

Out, out, brief candle!
Life's but a walking shadow,
A poor player that struts and frets his hour upon the stage, and then is heard no more:
It is a tale told by an idiot, full of sound and fury, signifying nothing.

William Shakespeare, *Macbeth*

Or, if you prefer a more modern observation from the other side of the Atlantic 'pond':

Y'know – Babylon once had two million people in it, and all we know about 'em is
the names of the kings and some copies of wheat contracts and … the sale of slaves.
Yet every night all those families sat down to supper, and the father came home
from work, and the smoke went up the chimney, same as here.

Thornton Wilder, *Our Town*

As we drove back to our hotel in Urfa, I scribbled away, trying to describe the day's adventures in my notebook as the others nodded off. The vehicle bumped and eddied its way through country roads in definite need of highway TLC and a random memory just popped into my consciousness. All of a sudden, I was mentally teleported back to 1966 and I would have been 11 years old, when my father gave me a present I've never forgotten. It was an illustrated book of science, entitled *The Universe of Galileo and Newton*, which I read and re-read many times, visually feasting on the marvellous illustrations. But I remember so well that exhilarating world you enter as an 11-year-old: a world of trailblazing scientific discovery presented in such a manner that captures you hook, line and sinker. This book also underscored the significant fact whereby science expands and refines its body of knowledge by following a pathway of learning and innovation from those who have gone before. This revered volume still holds pride of place on my bookcase today.

Of course, no internet back then in the far-off 1960s, so books for me had become a well-established firmament in my young life, satisfying a deep craving to seek out new knowledge coupled with the thrill in chasing after it. Not only that but books for me served as a means of escape to a universe of the imagination where one was free to dwell and to do as one pleased as a child. To me, books have always been a wondrous thing. Permit me to quote the following from the scientific sage, Carl Sagan, who said of books:

> *What an astonishing thing a book is. It's a flat object made from a tree with flexible parts on which are imprinted lots of funny dark squiggles but one glance at it and you're inside the mind of another person. Maybe somebody dead for thousands of years across the millennia. An author is speaking clearly and silently inside your head directly to you. Writing is perhaps the greatest of human inventions binding together people who never knew each other. Citizens of distant epochs. Books break the shackles of time.*[21]

And yet all those years ago, my father must have seen me with my nose in a book and he took me aside one day telling me something that has always remained as a firm fixture in my brain after more than a half a century. As an academic in TCD and a bibliophile of the first order, my father's words struck me as a bit weird, even as a kid, when he said how learning doesn't always have to come from books and that I should be ready to learn from life's experiences, the places I've been to, the people I've encountered, the things I've seen, the mistakes I'll make, the successes and setbacks in my life – in fact, to learn from everything.

Very much a statement of the 'bleedin' obvious', I grant you, but for the 11-year-old version of me all those years ago it was such an eye-opener of a home truth that was uttered when my immature brain was in 'receive mode'. I'm so thankful my father squeezed wide open that universe of childish reasoning so as to enable me to develop a more resilient self.

> *when young*
> *learning how to learn*
> *is a key*
> *to understanding*
> *in one's lifetime*

Back in the present in Northern Mesopotamia at our hotel, we said goodbye to Murad until the morning.

After an opportunity to freshen up and change for dinner, we made our way to a restaurant with a difference. It turned out to be a traditional Urfa evening with a distinctive Ottoman flavour in terms of the food on the menu and, as an added delight, the live music and song enjoyed during and after our meal. It was a *sira geçesi* (traditional banquet) evening.

The restaurant was decorated in time-honoured Ottoman fashion and we sat on the floor, surrounded by an abundance of cushions. We dined elegantly, with food served to us on silver dishes. Other families were present and we listened to a small orchestra who treated us to some local music and song. It may have been a bit touristy, perhaps, but it was good to have our hunger satisfied with delicious food Urfa-style, except that only soft drinks were available – no alcohol in this establishment. By this stage, even I was picking up on the fact that each city we were visiting so far had its own distinctive cuisine and now we were fortunate to be experiencing a taste of the food of this region.

Afterwards, calling on reserves of superhuman energy we young fogies possess in heaps, we ventured off in search of an iconic Urfa landmark, Zaleeha Park: a park with a legend attached.

Once, long ago, there was a young woman named Zaleeha, daughter of King Nemrut (remember him?). It so happened that the young lady had committed some misdeed and for this her father had condemned her to die. Not just any old death mind you, but death by burning. Yikes. But, somehow, Zaleeha acquired magical powers in just the nick of time before her demise and so she was able to change the fires of her execution into water filled with fish. So, in memory of this bittersweet legend, the people of Urfa have created for themselves this huge park replete with ponds and waterways and all filled with carp.

At this late hour in Ramadan, Zaleeha Park was buzzing with activity and many families were having picnics.

The four of us moseyed over to a quiet corner in the park and over a lemonade or two, we ruminated over the riches of the past we were encountering and learning so much about.

As it ticked well into the small hours, thanks to ample floodlighting, we could admire the grandeur of the imposing ancient walls of this city which are doubled in thickness in the manner constructed by the Abbasids of the 9th century CE. I remember picturing myself being present in Urfa 1,200 years previously when these walls were being built from scratch, the sounds of the work in progress, the voices of the men labouring away, the echo of the constant toing and froing of the many souls associated with this great enterprise and what it was like for the populace at large to live in this city.

A final thought on civilisation, as you do, when laying one's head on the pillow back at the hotel, I was reminded of:

Our revels now are ended. These our actors,
As I foretold you, were all spirits, and
Are melted into air, into thin air:
And like the baseless fabric of this vision,
The cloud-capp'd tow'rs, the gorgeous palaces,
The solemn temples, the great globe itself,
Yea, all which it inherit, shall dissolve,
And, like this insubstantial pageant faded,
Leave not a rack behind. We are such stuff
As dreams are made on; and our little life
Is rounded with a sleep.

William Shakespeare, *The Tempest*, Prospero, Act IV, Scene I

⌘ Some final thoughts

It came to my attention in January 2023 that a further site, Karahan Tepe, has been discovered some 80 km (50 miles) to the east of Göbeklitepe, displaying similar archaeological traits to the latter. It is believed that Karahan Tepe also has megaliths aligned with the cosmos, similar to Göbeklitepe.

For further details, please see work by Andrew Collins, 'Karahan Tepe: Göbekli Tepe's Sister Site – Another Temple of the Stars?'[22]

In his ground-breaking book, *Prehistory Decoded*, Martin Sweatman of the University of Edinburgh argues that early human societies had advanced knowledge encoded in their symbolic art and architecture, such as Göbeklitepe. These structures and artworks recorded astronomical information, with references to cataclysmic events like the Younger Dryas. By decoding these symbols, Sweatman believes we can gain insights into the beliefs and societal organisation of ancient civilisations. He proposes a universal system of astronomical symbolism across prehistoric cultures, challenging traditional views and highlighting early humans' advanced scientific understanding. This theory suggests that early humans were more advanced intellectually than previously thought.

It is conceivable that evidence emerging from Karahan Tepe, Göbeklitepe and other archaeological sites of similar vintage elsewhere may prove to be highly significant and give rise to a rethink of human history. As more facts come to light from these ancient locations, a more complete picture of the societies that constructed these megalithic monuments is emerging, suggesting a much more complex mindset on the part of these peoples of long ago. Not only that but the sophisticated design and layout of these sites would suggest these societies possessed a highly developed understanding of science, mathematics, astronomy and engineering.

Also, the presence of stone circles and other ancient remains at Karahan Tepe and Göbeklitepe, and even further afield at Boncuklu Tarla in Mardin Province – which is thought to date back even further than 12,000 years – all present a challenging counter-argument to the long-accepted archaeological theorising about what was the main push leading to the development of complex societies.

*Uruk
A city in ancient Mesopotamia, the remains of which are now located in Iraq.

*Ur-shanabi
The ferryman of the Hubur, the river of the dead in Mesopotamian legend.

*Stele
A rectangular prehistoric stone slab sometimes bearing an inscription or an illustration that has been incorporated into a monument.

Remains of Harran – further archaeological excavation is planned.

The distinctive beehive-shaped dwellings in Harran.

Dromedary (one-humped) camel spotted in the vicinity of Harran.

Ancient city walls on elevated ground in the distance, Urfa.

Shaded walkway beside the Urfa Archaeological Museum.

Tour guide, Murad (left) gesturing while discussing what life was like in ancient times, Urfa Archaeological Museum.

Full-sized models of megaliths from Göbeklitepe, Urfa Archaeological Museum.

Murad pointing out the Fertile Crescent, Urfa Archaeological Museum.
Ak Deniz is Turkish for Mediterranean Sea, *Kızıl Deniz* for Red Sea and *Kara Deniz* for Black Sea.

Column base, made from limestone, Islamic period, found near Harran, Urfa Archaeological Museum.

Limestone column element, Islamic period, Urfa Archaeological Museum.

Replica of stone carving of wild life and other symbolism, Göbeklitepe, Urfa Archaeological Museum.

Limestone tombstone, Islamic Age, Urfa Archaeological Museum.

Limestone baptismal font; Byzantine Era, Urfa Archaeological Museum.

Amazon warrior mosaic, Urfa Mosaic Museum.

Kizilkoyun Necropolis, the Red Sheep City of the Dead, Urfa. Note modern housing at the top.

Hotel El Ruha Grotto. Nearby is the birthplace of Abraham, Urfa.

Traditional musicians, Urfa.

Göbeklitepe, part of the excavated archaeological site, under a protective covering. An elevated walkway facilitates an excellent view of the various artefacts on display.

Part of the protective covering over the excavated section of the archaeological site of Göbeklitepe shown with an external wooden walkway.

Partly-excavated area elsewhere on the Göbeklitepe site. Only 5 per cent of the entire ancient complex has been unearthed.

The Mesopotamian Plain, as seen from Göbeklitepe.

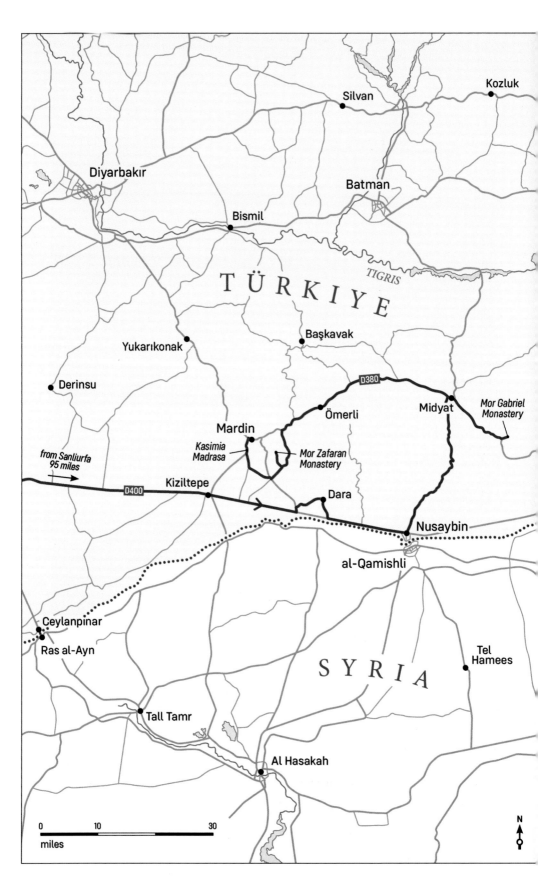

TUESDAY 28TH MAY 2019

Exploring a rich cultural heritage underground,
at ground level and on top of a hill

cultural threads
distant from us
in place and time
will find a way
to connect

PROPOSED ITINERARY:
▷ Leave Urfa and onwards to Dara via Kiziltepe
▷ Dara and Zindan Cisterns
▷ Lunch in Midyat
▷ Nusaybin
▷ Mor Gabriel Monastery
▷ Drive to Midyat, followed by Mor Zafaran Monastery and Kasimia Madrasa
▷ Mardin

On this, Day 6, we were greeted as always with a smile by our driver and tour guide. At 9am, we set off for the historical site of Dara, some 200 km (125 miles) distant. Murad told us that our drive would be just under two and a half hours and we'd pass through the town of Kiziltepe (Redhill), itself an ancient place of archaeological interest. Our route would be a straightforward one as we headed along the now familiar paved rite of passage, the D-400.

You see, coming from Dublin, when I first heard Murad mention Dara, I thought that perhaps there might be an Irish connection with this part of Northern Mesopotamia. Hey, that's not such a crazy idea as I've read that back in the mid-19th century, the Ottoman Sultan Abdulmajid had been recorded providing assistance to the starving Irish nation during the Great Famine of 1847. He despatched help in the form of cash (a donation of £10,000 was given which would be the equivalent of £1.2m approximately in today's money) and food, the latter arriving in three ships which docked in Drogheda having been refused permission by the British authorities to anchor in the port of Dublin. There is debate about the donation given as it has been intimated the benevolent Sultan wished to give more than £10,000 but that the British authorities prevented this happening; so far, no firm evidence has yet come to light to support this interpretation of history.

A variation on the theme of a 'recollections may vary' version of past events, perhaps.

But my spring-sprong brain leapt off on a tangent as our tour guide continued to hold forth. What came to my mind was someone I'd known, a chap by the name of (the late) Paul Darragh (an Irish alternative on the spelling of Dara) who was two classes ahead of me at school in Dublin. While still relatively young he became a famous show jumper, riding horses in international competitions and, joy of joys, was a member of the Irish show jumping team that won the illustrious Aga Khan trophy three years on the trot (please excuse the pun, it was intentional) in 1977–79. Those were the years when Irish show jumping reigned supreme.

Now, you'd think I'd be merciful here and spare you more of my continued musings re. the Irish connection with the name Dara or Darragh for that matter. Well, in a word: no. You see the link with Paul Darragh continues in another unbelievable way. OK, bear with me as we go back over 40 years to 1980, when I lived for two years in northern Greece and made friends with a Greek chap called Harry L., with whom I played tennis on the courts of Aristotle University of Thessaloniki and who was a skier of international standing. He has remained a close chum to this day I am happy to say and now runs a successful business in Athens. His wife Emmanouela is into horses in a big way, running her own stable just outside the nation's capital and she has also represented Greece in show jumping at international level, including the Olympics. It happened that my wife and I were in Greece in 2018 and we dropped in on Harry and Emmanouela and their delightful son. While in conversation, the subject of horse riding came up and, by the by, I mentioned I had known Paul Darragh, the famous equestrian figure. On hearing this, Emmanouela exclaimed with a combination of surprise and delight that coincidentally Paul had been her trainer when she'd gone to live and work in Ireland to hone her show jumping skills some time past. I remember thinking what a small world we live in when hearing of this shared connection – all down to my hearing the word 'dara' and it setting off this astonishing train of thought plucked from memory.

When looking into the early history of Northern Mesopotamia, Dara is a Sumerian word meaning 'blood' and also the Sumerian god, Enki, was known as Dara-mah.

Dara is written in Babylonian cuneiform text as follows:[23]

Dara in Northern Mesopotamia first gets a write-up in the history books at the beginning of the 6th century, 503 to be exact, and the Romans – yes, they were still very much around – were in need of a new garrison town on the eastern fringes of their Empire which bordered Persia. Their previous stronghold, Assida, to the north – now known as Diyarbakir (also on our itinerary) – had fallen to the Persians and the Romans were in a bit of a jam sorting out where to station their troops at risk of attack from their Persian foe. After some searching for the 'right' place, the military planners decided on locating their new army HQ in the small village of Dara near some hills and the River Cordes (from the ancient Greek Κόρδης [Kordis]), a tributary of the Euphrates. In Roman eyes, this was an ideal spot to defend against attack, so plans were drawn up and the village was expanded, becoming a thriving and elegant military town of 20,000 people. The town was protected by high walls interspersed with towers that ringed the entire new urban setup with a flourishing *agora* (market), public baths, porticoes, storehouses and cisterns – six of these cisterns have been discovered, of which two have been excavated. In this enlarged Dara, there was also a palace, churches, columns of Anastasius (along with the Roman emperor Justinian, as both leaders had overseen the design, construction and repair of this new town) and many other buildings. According to the Roman custom of the day and being Greek-speaking*, Dara was renamed as Anastasiopolis in honour of the incumbent emperor.

Within a four- to five-year period in the 6th century, Dara had been transformed into a fortress outpost of the Roman Empire in the north Mesopotamian Plain only a few miles from the frontier with its powerful Persian rival. In addition, Dara or Anastasiopolis as it was then called, became a major trading point with goods flowing in both directions, east and west along this detour on the famous Silk Road. Not only that but Anastasiopolis also served as an important diplomatic reception point where embassies from, say, neighbouring Persia, would present themselves and be met by government officials who would escort them onwards within this eastern section of the Roman Empire.

When doing further research on Dara, I was grateful when I came across references to a Roman writer rejoicing in the name of Procopius of Caeserea (now called Qaysaria in northern Israel) living in the 6th century. Procopius travelled to Dara on a number of occasions and recorded details of his visits entitled *De Aedificiis* (*Of Buildings*), but 'Buildings' might be a more suitable translation and also in a second book, *De Bello Persico* (*The Persian War*). His writings also include descriptions of the major works carried out there to convert it into a strongly defended military garrison town with trading and ambassadorial facilities thrown in as well.

The city of Dara is situated on the edge of the desert, and it is strongly fortified by a wall which extends for more than six miles in circumference. The wall of Dara is built of stone, and it is strengthened by numerous towers and bastions. It is so high that it is impossible for an enemy to climb over it, and so thick that it cannot be destroyed by any siege engine. The city of Dara is a place of great strategic importance, as it guards the eastern frontier of the Byzantine Empire and controls the trade routes that run through Mesopotamia. During the siege of Dara, the Byzantine defenders employed various tactics to resist the Sassanid attacks, including using catapults to launch fireballs at the enemy and building counter-walls to block their advance.

'Procopius and Dara', by Brian Croke and James Crow, *The Journal of Roman Studies*, 1983, Vol. 73, pp. 143–59 and *De Aedificiis* and *De Bello Persico*, by Procopius of Caesarea et al.

As the minibus ate up the miles on the D-400, the atmosphere that Tuesday morning was one of great excitement tinged with anticipation. There was a great deal of discussion about the various historical places we'd been to so far associated with different civilisations. But Murad sounded a word of warning, as it were, as he wished to dispel any starry-eyed notions of Mesopotamia the four of us travellers might have been harbouring. Our guide didn't shy away from the fact that much of the ancient history of Mesopotamia is unfortunately written in blood and there has existed since the dawn of time a constant tension between the different population groups coexisting in this part of the world.

Ordinary people had to contend with extreme violence, political shenanigans, hatred, war, genocide, enforced poverty, lack of tolerance and persecution of people with different beliefs and also forced labour or slavery. And other unpleasant stuff.

But it was not all bad. There was, however, an overarching existential counterweight to all this as the Sumerian people, for example, had founded the oldest known urban civilisation in the world as far back as 5,500 BCE. Over the next 3,500 years or so, the Sumerians established advances in science, technology, social evolution, astronomy, governance, art, culture, law and medicine.

Yes, there was a strong hierarchical stratification to the society and yes, there were slaves and a privileged elite, but the free citizens, who comprised the majority of the population, did have freedoms and rights. They were permitted to own property and could also choose their livelihood, be it a profession, farming, government administration or commerce.

But like all good things, it did come to an end. That never-ending cycle of ἔρως καὶ θάνατος (*eros kay thanatos*, translated from the ancient Greek as love and death) being a universal signifier of the positive and negative driving forces in human progress since earliest times has continued. But as you will have seen, I have not confined myself to this part of the world in terms of outlook. I always want to look further over other horizons.

The concept of the relationship between love and death as driving forces in humanity exist in various other cultures, although the specific terms used may differ and it's important to note the nuances and cultural interpretations may vary.

China: one notable concept is the duality of Yin and Yang, representing opposing yet complementary forces in the universe. Love and death can be seen as part of this larger framework of opposing forces. This I remember well from my schooldays, as my former French teacher, Monsieur L., in Dublin, would regale us frequently about Yin and Yang and the associated philosophy.

On one occasion, he played a neat linguistic trick on us: in that ancient time of the 1960s when reel-to-reel audio tapes reigned supreme, Monsieur L. would avail of this bit of kit to teach us French. His usual technique was to stop the reel mid-flow when some (French) person was speaking and ask for a victim, I mean class member, to repeat. On this particular day, he set up the equipment and tape in the usual way and there was a discernible groan in the class as Monsieur L. always seemed to select tricky dialogues for us to work with. The tape was duly started but it was not French that emerged from the speaker; it sounded as if it might be Chinese. Our teacher paused the recording and said to our horror that we had to repeat what we heard. There then followed a bizarre exercise whereby some of us were expected to replicate the verbal output coming from this tape recorder. It proved really hard as every syllable uttered by the unknown foreign interlocutor was alien to us.

Monsieur L. then called a halt – much to our collective relief. With a deft hand, he swapped the reels over on the same machine and played it again. As if by magic, the French language was to be heard. So, we learnt a lesson I've retained to this day: French spoken backwards sounds just like Chinese.

India: the concepts of death and love are deeply interconnected with notions of life, rebirth and transcendence. Love can be associated with divine or spiritual love (*Bhakti*), while death is viewed as a transformative process leading to liberation or union with the divine. The cycles of life, death and rebirth are central to Indian philosophical traditions like Hinduism and Buddhism.

Japan: the concept of '*mono no aware*' explores the transient and poignant nature of existence. It involves an awareness of the impermanence of life and the appreciation of the beauty in that transience, often evoking a sense of both love and sorrow.

Ancient Egypt: the concepts of love and death were intertwined with their understanding of the afterlife. Love, in the form of devotion and affection, was essential for the soul's journey to the realm of the dead. Death, on the other hand, represented a transformation into the eternal realm and a continuation of existence.

Ancient Norse: the interplay between love and death can be seen in the stories of the gods and goddesses. The inevitability of death, as represented by the fate of the gods during *Ragnarok* ('Twilight of the Gods': final battle of the gods resulting in the destruction and rebirth of the world), is juxtaposed with the power of love and human connections that give meaning to life.

I've come to realise cultural interpretations of love and death may vary significantly around the world, and there may not be direct equivalents to the specific terms '*eros kay thanatos*' in every culture. However, exploring philosophical, spiritual and literary traditions of different cultures can reveal similar themes and ideas revolving around the fundamental aspects of love, life and mortality.

> *pathways*
> *to civilisation*
> *are etched into*
> *blood-soaked maps*
> *why?*

I would add another question: with all these civilisations existing not only in Mesopotamia but also around the world over many thousands of years, why all the suffering and bloodshed? I mean, why can't civilisations be civilised?

As we drove on from Kiziltepe to Dara, we observed that the hills surrounding the area we were passing through had a distinctive red hue and we thought this might be due to iron ore in the soil. Murad said that there was also a gold mine nearby.

A little later, we arrived at the ancient city of Dara. The sky was cloudless and the sun shone but thank goodness it wasn't as hot as the previous day and I was grateful that a light breeze was wafting its way over us as we walked from our minibus. I looked about us and observed that we were deep in the countryside on a quiet road. Close by was a delightful apparition of the oleander flower in all its pinkish-red glory. On the other side of the road, I spotted a house with an unusual birdlike mural painted in bold colours on the side and on the front elevation. I wondered if it signified anything.

I asked Murad about this and he confirmed that it was a peacock: a sacred Yazidi religious symbol signifying immortality and that we would be seeing numerous examples of this emblem in the area we'd be travelling through.

By the open entrance to the site of Dara, I saw a small wooden hut with an official from the state museums and antiquities department standing by. He was smiling and welcomed us warmly in Turkish. Murad told us that we could go right ahead as there was no entrance fee.

First thing I noticed was that it was quiet, as we appeared to be the only visitors present in this ancient place. A wide, light-coloured pebbled pathway with parched grassy areas on either side snaked its way ahead of us, veering to the right and then was lost to view between golden-coloured outcroppings of bare rock. This dramatic stonework appeared to have sheared sides and was well distributed around a surreal landscape hemmed in by higher ground. A distinctive yellow-brownish limestone covered most of the area.

Just inside the entrance was a big notice in Turkish with details about Dara, with an English translation attached, for which I was grateful. The sign was informative with handy illustrations mentioning, among other things, that there were two ancient churches on the site and the existence of a number of cisterns. But the one thing that jumped out was the intriguing mention that Dara could be much older – 2,300 years old in fact – as there is a school of thought which speculates that it was first built by the Sassanid king, King Darius, who reigned in the 300s BCE. That would have been about 800 years before the Roman era and its development as a military garrison as described above by Procopius of Caeserea. An intriguing historical anomaly, perhaps in need of further 'digging', as it were, to uncover the truth about the origins of Dara.

It is interesting to note that Dara had largely become forgotten until the mid-1980s when work was started to excavate this place, as it had become concealed under a pile of earth. Since then, archaeologists have been hard at it uncovering the ancient story of this place but only about 10–15 per cent of the entire site has been dug out.

The one noticeable feature about many of the rocks is that they've big holes cut into them. This is because Dara had served as a necropolis (meaning 'city of the dead', as also seen in Urfa), i.e. a graveyard on a massive scale both when the city flourished during the 6th and into the 7th century CE and then even after when Dara had fallen into disuse from the 14th century CE onwards. One of the reasons for burial in this manner was that a large number of the deceased, as I read in the historic record, were Zoroastrians and also followers of the god Mithras, supposedly born from rock – this latter belief system was related to Zoroastrianism. These religious rites forbade burial in the earth lest it caused contamination and so the dead bodies had to be interred in the rocks above ground. Even though conversion to Christianity had taken place in this area some 2,000 years ago, the local people still practised the old customs, maintaining a dualistic spiritual creed for hundreds of years until well into Islamic times, when those ancient practices were considered to be pagan and no longer observed.

Let me describe what it was like to be there in Dara. We continued on our way through this ancient site and our shoes crunched over the pebbles. I was walking down a silent avenue with buildings carved from the solid rock between two to three storeys tall on both sides of me, some leaning at a jaunty angle and every so often I could see there were two parallel rows of holes big enough to accommodate sarcophagi carved into the vertical limestone. At one point, I spotted a freestanding rectangular boulder of the same rock that's about the height of a double-decker bus, which has been cut through entirely from two opposite sides creating an eerie open-windowed sculpture that framed a clear arched view of the sky with its vibrant blueness that would not have looked out of place in a painting by Titian, Vermeer or Hockney.

Murad showed us around a very early Christian church and an ossuary (where bones of the deceased are interred) – both of which had also been carved out of the rock. Apart from the inner space of what used to be the church there is not much to see but the ossuary, which is called the Great Catacomb according to a helpful sign positioned nearby. This has been turned into a compact museum with glass-surfaced walkways that permit one to view the skeletal remains of some 3,000 people buried there and our mood became reflective as we passed through.

The sun had now risen to its zenith and it was turning out to be a scorcher of a day. This was when Rashida's umbrella made another appearance to protect her from those pesky ultra-violet rays. At one point, our driver walked up to Rashida to seek shelter under her brolly. Whilst we drank from our water bottles to keep dehydration at bay, we did feel for Murad who was fasting and didn't touch a drop but who didn't slacken the pace. I reckoned the temperature must have been well above 30 degrees Celsius – years of living under the constancy of a hot sun in Saudi Arabia does give one the knack of gauging such extreme levels of heat.

We didn't see any remnants of the old city walls or towers of Dara – that pleasure awaits us in the future.

As we exited Dara via the main gate we had gone through about an hour and a half previously, a train of thought struck me. I recalled field trips back in the 1970s as a hard-up student in Ireland exploring the geology, geography and history from around different parts of the country. The weather was invariably grey, damp and cold as we stumbled through muddy fields in Co. Kerry to view leftovers from the Ice Age, such as an erratic* or a glacial lake*, or when we clambered over Pre-Cambrian* rock formations in Co. Galway my fellow students seemed to know so much about or as I gazed in stupefaction at how the distinctive Carboniferous* limestone karst* landscape of the Burren in Co. Clare had been formed 325 million years ago. At the end of many of those excursions, hot whiskies proved an invaluable pick-me-up when recovering from the inclement climactic conditions we'd been expected to wade through and I can remember thinking, nay dreaming, if I would ever visit sites of historical or scientific importance in a warm, dry and sunnier clime. Come to think about it, it has taken half a century for that wish to come true in Northern Mesopotamia. About time.

After a short stroll, we entered a village where we came across areas of open ground with what I presume to be the detritus of old Dara in the form of numerous rocks of assorted sizes and shapes scattered about the place as if tossed there by some careless giant. Our arrival excited interest in the neighbourhood, as I saw signs of 'curtain twitching' and small children approached us smiling. Some of the kids spoke to us and the language didn't sound Arabic or Turkish, so I deduced it might be Kurdish; I made a mental note to ask Murad later and when I did he confirmed my guess.

After a 15-minute walk, we arrived at what can be best described as a low-built, circular-roofed structure lying straight on the ground with nothing apparently underneath, made from the same limestone rock of the region except on this occasion each bit of this sedimentary material has been roughly cut into irregular blocks, cemented together into this weird bit of round-roofed architecture. This was totally unexpected.

I took a closer look and it dawned on me that this must be the actual entrance to the Zindan (Turkish for 'dungeon') Cistern, as a low wall guided us to a series of steps that descended beneath this circular roof which was now overhead. We walked down the many solid but uneven stone steps to the cistern which is 35 m (115 ft) below ground. The four of us took extreme care with the countless uneven steps, as losing one's footing wasn't an option, considering there was no handrail or other means of protecting yourself against a nasty tumble. A group of kids, however, made light of our concerns with health and safety as they ran up and down the steps without a care in the world as they played a game.

When we joined our guide at a galleried landing about a third of the way down, we were all in agreement in expressing our surprise that we would never have located the entrance to the cistern. Murad laughed as he replied that this would have been uppermost in the minds of the original city planners in the early 6th century CE going about their work guided by a strategic way of thinking. Concealment from the enemy – in this case, the neighbouring Sassanid Empire – was key to protecting Dara's precious water supply from the River Cordes in case of attack or siege.

Roman engineering skill came to the fore; they succeeded in diverting the River Cordes by means of a canal, then the water flowed into Dara and it could be diverted to the cavernous cisterns underground away from enemy eyes.

But that's not all. The Romans realised that by solving one problem they had created another: the threat of flooding now reared its ugly head so that the newly developed city was at risk. Unperturbed, they came up with another crafty design solution by creating an arched dam to ensure a constant flow of water which also protected Dara from the danger of inundation.

You could say our puzzlement in trying to locate this cistern just now was exactly what the Romans had intended 1,500 years previously in trying to confound those with an evil eye on the source of the city's water supply. And, of course, if one cistern was discovered or put out of action, there were still five more to supply the good people of Dara. You could say that Dara was following, therefore, the military maxim of planning for the worst and hoping for the best while the theory and practice of holding something in reserve also was very much part and parcel of the thought processes of those in charge of this new city renamed as Anastasiopolis.

We saw two of the cisterns and I am glad to say that there was ample illumination provided with a subtle touch that added to the drama of the experience, as when I stood on the floor of the first cistern, I gazed upwards and was struck by the scale of the engineering involved.

After the cisterns, we strolled for a further 1.5 km (1 mile) down some pathways, past more houses and even across a field or two until we arrived at the *agora* – the market place. We walked along a bit of what would have been their local high street, called Palace Street, now in ruins. In keeping with the quality of city design, it was a fully paved thoroughfare 5.5 m (18 ft) wide with a gentle camber still evident and you could make out the former regular floorplans of the shops which would have sat on either side of the street. At this point, I took a selfie of sorts but this was different as it captured only my left arm where my hand was touching one of the rocks from a long-lost shop that was once on Palace Street. My thoughts ranged back in time nearly 1,500 years and I let my mind create an imagined scene with this shop as a well kitted-out retail outlet in the year 509. I visualised it to be full of wares for sale and the owner inside with perhaps a shop assistant or two. I pictured the shop owner stepping out onto the street and shouting out what was on offer to the passing throng of people and the whole place bustling with noise and activity, as several uniformed Roman legionnaires just given leave were in the process of hunting out some bargains when buying gifts for their loved ones back home. On top of the clamour of the market place, I could almost smell the scent of saffron, myrrh, roses, cloves and thyme permeating the air around me.

How those soldiers of long ago might have looked on their forthcoming furlough with eager anticipation, resignation or dread, depending on their individual circumstances.

My mind darted back home to some local shopping areas close to us where we now live in London and even farther back where I grew up in Dublin in the 1960s and early 70s and I wondered what remnants of these commercial centres would be picked over by someone 1,500 years into the future – the year 3523. What would those yet-to-appear archaeologists (or the future equivalent) make of our era, our culture, our civilisation? What fragmentary evidence would survive? Think about it, there's so much happening in the news, what with Covid-19 and the fallout from the pandemic whether medical, social, economic or political. Brexit-related issues still flick across the airwaves in the UK and then there's all that stuff about the environment and how we're poisoning our planet. Further thorny topics that dominate our lives and the media right now are numerous but let me add a few more: the continuing unresolved problems in the Middle East; Black Lives Matter and issues related to sex and gender. But out of all this plethora of stuff crowding our finite existences at this moment, what would be discovered 1, 2, 3 or 5,000 years from now?

And lo and behold, on 24th February 2022, the Russians invaded Ukraine – for a second time – following their first incursion back in 2014. This was not some low-key skirmish; this was outright war waged by a certain despot in Moscow intent on returning all the territory of Ukraine to the Russian fold. This conflict still rages on as Ukraine, under the remarkable leadership of President Volodymyr Zelenskyy, is holding its own in its existential fight for survival against the aggressor. Here's hoping against hope this is not the prelude to World War Three and the annihilation of life as we know it.

All this crams our existence at the moment with nerve-shredding regularity, sometimes to breaking point. This maelstrom of shit in the world jogs my memory about W.B. Yeats in his memorable poem, The Second Coming, where he says, "Things fall apart, the centre cannot hold". Even though these words were penned over 100 years ago by Ireland's first Nobel laureate in literature after the First World War but just before the Irish Civil War of 1922, as I write this book in 2023, I am struck by the connection with the problems we face today and am further reminded of the British/ Turkish author Elif Shafak, who has written: "Ours is the age of contagious anxiety. We feel overwhelmed by events around us, by injustice, by suffering, by an endless feeling of crisis", from her book, *How To Stay Sane In An Age Of Division* (2020).

Our stopover at the remarkable age-old city of Dara and the Zindan Cisterns concluded, we got back into our minivan and continued motoring along the now-familiar D-400 on our way to have lunch in Midyat before heading on to the Mor Gabriel Monastery. Our journey in history, through history and about history continued. As we headed further east, Murad informed us we'd be passing through Nusaybin. That's when we came within a stone's throw of the frontier separating Türkiye from Syria. As we hurtled along the motorway, I gauged that it couldn't have been more than 100 m (330 ft) away from us at certain points. Between us and the 3 m (<10 ft) high border wall were fallow fields and this barrier runs for about 810 km (503 miles), separating Syria and Türkiye. For years up to the start of the Syrian Civil War in 2011, this had been a porous border with smuggling and people passing to and fro availing of the numerous tunnels in the area.

Then, in 2015, Türkiye initiated a major wall-building programme, with financial contributions from the EU. The purpose was to stem the tide of refugees fleeing Syria. As it happens, Türkiye is now host to about 3.6 million Syrian refugees officially but there is anecdotal evidence to suggest this figure might be higher – as previously mentioned on Day 3 in Gaziantep.

Murad reminded us that only a few years ago when he was in the area, he saw the ravages of war.

As we drove on, we gazed into Syria and in the distance could make out thick smoke billowing skywards from a village surrounded by farmland. It was an eerie sight and we speculated as to whether this fire had an innocent genesis or was it something more sinister. I feared the latter, as media reports hammered home the news of continued military activity in Syria. This wretched civil war that has dragged on for almost a decade shows no sign of ending and the misery continues for the people affected. We all expressed our sadness with a heavy sigh at the level of death, suffering, displacement of people and destruction that has occurred in Syria up to now. Even if hostilities were to finish tomorrow (a highly unlikely prospect), it would take many years for the country to fully recover from this abominable bloodletting. As the old saying goes, civil war is anything but civil.

Border: hey, that is a word that loudly resonates with me as I grew up in Ireland with 'The Border' very much an integral part of my cultural landscape. By 'Border' I mean of course the 499-km (310-mile) boundary separating the Republic of Ireland from Northern Ireland, the latter being a six-county member of the United Kingdom with the remaining 26 counties of the Republic being also referred to as the 'South'.

There was added significance for us as a family, as my mother was from the Republic with Wexford and Dublin ancestry whereas my father was from the North, where he regarded the three neighbouring counties of Donegal (Republic of Ireland), Londonderry/Derry and Tyrone (Northern Ireland) as his hinterland.

Back in the distant late 1960s and all through the 70s, I can recall 'The Border' being reported on a near daily basis in the Irish media during the period which came to be known as The Troubles. I wondered as a teenager if it would ever end. There was all the political chicanery, plus the incessant ravages to the physical fabric of the province aided by arson, the bullet and the explosive, and of course, the worst of all, the human suffering and bloodshed which filled many ballistic headlines with tragic monotony over 30 years. A nemesis of the cruellest kind had established itself as a means to settle long-held grievances and contemporary scores. Vile retribution was now the order of the day, not only in the Border area but also around Ulster. And this wretched mayhem remained as our daily diet of bloodiness until the signing of the Good Friday Agreement in 1998.

That accord was a momentous event endowed with such hope and optimism for the future. You could almost feel the widespread cathartic sigh of relief as centuries of bitterness and carnage were laid aside. The Border which had morphed into a tainted gateway into Northern Ireland riven with festering hatred and division must have torn at the soul of anyone connected with that part of the island of Ireland or the United Kingdom, depending on your political, religious or social perspective. And with this historic Agreement, in a master stroke of diplomacy, The Border which had hitherto acted as a divisive separator between the Republic of Ireland and Northern Ireland, was all but banished as customs barriers, border crossings and the contentious military watch towers were all done away with. No more physical evidence of The Border. For the first time in my life, a new era had come into existence, giving every semblance of a united Ireland, even though the political Lego-work of the past century still remained in situ, more or less.

let our hearts
be
without borders
embracing
the other

I believe I first learnt about borders thanks to the German nanny my sister and I had at home in Dublin back in 1961. Fraulein Anita K. was a young, friendly Berliner and she was sad when she told us about her native city being divided between East and West. I recall Anita showing us pictures of the Berlin Wall. It made a deep impression on me because even as a six-year-old, I came to realise a border can cause pain and division. An abiding memory from then is seeing a photo of a man in tears standing by his home in West Berlin, peering through a recently erected high barbed-wire fence separating him from his place of work, now off-limits just metres away in East Berlin.

In addition to my experience of how borders impinge on our lives, both Suat and Feray's parents were affected by border issues related to their original homeland in Cyprus riven by the Greek and Turk communities at loggerheads with each other. Both families of Feray and Suat sought refuge oversees and Britain became their home.

This thorny subject of national boundaries is well covered by the Bulgarian author Kapka Kassabova in her book *Border*, which describes the border zone shared between three neighbouring countries: Bulgaria, Türkiye and Greece. As you read her account, you soon realise it is so much more than a travelogue by an author returning to the borderlands where she grew up after a gap of 25 years.

Part-autobiographical and part-poetic, this writer brings to life the numerous people she meets on her extensive journeys in many border locations. In each of the three nations she passes through she also draws on local folklore and even spirituality that is special to these areas. What I really liked about her book was the fact she gave me to understand that there are more similarities than differences amongst people.

Coming as I do from Ireland with both British/Protestant and Irish/Catholic roots, I had seen ample evidence of bloody internecine conflict during the first 24 years of my life in Ireland and then in other places I have been to; for example, Greece and Türkiye, with the enduring enmity between these two nations, and then Saudi Arabia, with the never-ending conflicts in the Middle East.

We exited the D-400. As we drew into Nusaybin, the driver turned off the main road and we went into the centre of town. We sat there parked for several minutes as the driver went off on some errand. I looked about me and took in my surroundings.

Nusaybin, previously called Nisibis, has a fascinating history. Formerly, it was part of the Achaemenid, Hellenic, Seleucid, Roman, Parthian and Sassanid Empires at various intervals where its strategic location meant that it has faced being taken and retaken by different armies.

Strabo, the Greek historian (64/63 BCE–24 CE), in his famous book entitled *Geography*, described Nisibis as a fortress at a strategic spot on the route serving Armenia and Mesopotamia. Later, the Roman historian and soldier Ammianus Marcellinus (330–391/400 CE), who depicts Nisibis as a vital stronghold of the Sassanid Empire in his major tome, *Res Gestae*.

In late antiquity*, Nisibis was in possession of a renowned place of Christian learning, the East Syrian School of Edessa (aka Nisibis). The school was associated with the Syriac branch of Christianity and flourished over a period of 300 years from 4th–7th century CE where theology, philosophy, science and literature were taught within an environment that was simultaneously intellectually rigorous and nurturing. During its heyday, the school's sphere of influence was considerable and stretched in the west to Vivarium in Calabria in southern Italy where a monastery was established, through what is now Greece, Türkiye, Syria, Iraq and eastwards through Asia as far as Xi'an in China, where there was a monastery known as the Daqin Pagoda.

More recent history, however, indicates that Nusaybin is still beset with serious frontier issues and there is reportedly a minefield on the border between Türkiye and Syria.

As the French would say, *Plus ça change, plus c'est la même chose.*

That said, it was all warm sunshine and tranquillity during our early afternoon visit there. I could see shops, a garage, a bank, a mosque and a restaurant nearby. We must also have been near a school because as I looked to my left, I observed many boys and girls of differing ages dressed in their blue school uniform. The morning shift had obviously just finished and like kids all over the planet when school's out, they were happily meandering about the place and socialising, sometimes boisterously, with each other. It looked a very normal, happy sight. I then turned to my right and spotted a continuous high wall running along the side of a street with houses going right up to it and I could also see buildings on the other side of this barrier. I realised we were now within yards of the frontier between Türkiye and Syria, with the Syrian town of Qamishli on the other side of this wall. Another border.

We departed from Nusaybin and soon after arrived in the town of Midyat where we dined upstairs on a ho-hum lunch in the Simit Restaurant, part of a chain throughout Türkiye. A slight disappointment, as the cuisine we savoured en route was usually of a consistent high quality.

⛪ Mor Gabriel and Mor Zafaran Monasteries

We drove most of the 22.5 km (14 miles) separating Midyat and the Monastery of Mor Gabriel on the D-380 and arrived at our destination in a little under 30 minutes. The final approach was up a gently rising hill to the main entrance of the monastery, a very tall and imposing gate set between high walls: Murad had made the arrangements and we were expected.

We alighted from our vehicle and walked through an oasis of greenery shaded by the presence of sugar pine trees which formed a most welcome arch of protection from the sun. Then to an inner courtyard where another grand entrance came into view. We waited a little while, as we were due to be shown around by someone from within the monastery. The afternoon was advancing, the stinging heat of earlier had barely abated and a radiant blue sky still reigned over us. I couldn't help but notice an atmosphere that could be best described as serene, as there was no ambient noise except for the comforting presence of a welcome breeze that flowed over us and the sound of birdsong. We congregated beneath a Japanese pagoda tree to avail of the benign shade it provided and from this position I was able to see a partly open metal gate some 4.5 m (14.5 ft) in height. Above it was a plaque in light-coloured stone emblazoned with two crosses and in between was some cursive script that looked like an amalgam of Arabic and Hebrew. Beneath that was written in clear black Roman script: *Mor Gabriel Deyrulumur Manastiri 397*. I wondered what this inscription meant.

A young gentleman with a polite, friendly demeanour appeared at the large gate and, in excellent English, apologised for keeping us. Introductions were made and we learnt that our new guide was called Gabriel, who then ushered us into a secluded area of the monastery. Seeing our cameras, Gabriel told us it would be fine to take photos.

Gabriel confirmed that Mor Gabriel had been established 1,622 years ago in 397 when, according to tradition, two holy men, Samuel and Simon, founded the monastery after a dream of godly revelation commanding them to erect a house of prayer on the plateau called Tur Abdin. This is a hilly part of south-eastern Türkiye and the name, Tur Abdin, is derived from the Syriac language meaning 'mountain of the servants'. As Gabriel showed us around, we noticed that there were high inner walls with Syriac script much in evidence and carved over doorways. We passed through very robust-looking metal doors which led into inner courtyards that had every appearance of being sanctuaries of peace where fountains played. The green foliage set against the cream-coloured walls also made for a pleasing visual impact that was a delight to experience. When I asked Gabriel about the layout of the monastery, he said that Mor Gabriel had been constructed with the protection of the community of monks, nuns, students and other residents very much in mind.

We learnt that Mor Gabriel had been attacked on various occasions by invading armies over the years, including the Mongols under Temurlane who came in 1401. The monastery had possessed an extensive library but it was ransacked and many of the books were destroyed or stolen. Some of these volumes, Gabriel said, have now turned up in American libraries and at the British Museum in London. We also learnt about the Syriac Orthodox religion and how it has fared over the years, often coming under pressure which has threatened its existence. Our guide went on to say that there is a worldwide diaspora of people adhering to the Syriac Orthodox faith, with many congregations in Europe, Australia and the United States. More recently, a prolonged legal process involving the monastery and various departments of the Turkish government is further cause for concern for the people associated with Mor Gabriel. The matter awaits resolution.

Within this region there are 12 monasteries, of which only seven are fully functioning today, with the others having been abandoned or fallen into disuse.

There was an ascetic beauty about Mor Gabriel Monastery and we were all impressed by the quietly spoken and knowledgeable guide. One thing caught my eye on our walk through the various chapels and alcoves we were guided through: a faded painting which brought to mind Leonardo da Vinci's iconic scene from the history of Christianity, *The Last Supper*. Gabriel confirmed that we were looking at a copy, as the original is in Milan, northern Italy, and we talked about a controversy that has arisen over this artwork as it has been questioned if Mary Magdalene was among the disciples of Jesus Christ at this Last Supper. The controversy continues to this day.

The tour of Mor Gabriel over, we took our leave, thanking our guide Gabriel for making us all feel so welcome and for his illuminating tour.

We then made our way back to Midyat and I noted that the weather continued to be kind to us. It was uplifting to be able to enjoy cloudless skies as lots of vitamin D benefitted all of us.

Plans were devised to patronise the local market, to acquire a new hat for Suat and, most important, some local wine to be purchased. Once in Midyat, we immediately embarked on exploring the bazaar. Suitable headgear was obtained for Suat and then Feray and Rashida indulged in some retail therapy, buying small items of silver jewellery as gifts for family back home. Next, we headed off to a local wine merchant and, to our surprise, the store was open but unattended. We waited a few minutes and the proprietor returned. We joked with him that we hadn't run off with his best vintage! The shop owner greeted us warmly while making it clear that wine producers in Türkiye were coming under continued pressure from a number of quarters, as alcohol is frowned upon by some elements in Turkish society. A great pity as Suat and I are quite fond of Turkish wine and bought some of the local produce.

With the shopping gene satisfied, we set a course for Mor Zafaran Monastery, aka Mor Hananyo, a stone's throw from Mardin.

What is eye-catching about Mor Zafaran, located on top of a high hilly area overlooking the city of Mardin, is its stunning architecture. This site has been used as a place of worship for thousands of years – long pre-dating Christianity. Originally, there was a temple dedicated to the Sumerian sun god, Shamash, and this ancient temple was then incorporated into the structure of the monastery which has been made and remade over the centuries. There is evidence confirming it has had a spiritual connection from as long ago as 2,000 BCE.

Later, the Romans occupied the area, making the edifice more fortress-like, and this temple was adapted to a different system of worship in keeping with Roman religious practices. Subsequently, in 493 CE, Mor Zafaran Monastery began its existence and was built from the local yellow limestone rock that is plentiful throughout. It is a Syriac Christian place of prayer, contemplation and learning. It also provided a home to Syriac orphans and poor children of the neighbourhood while serving as a place to live for the monks and other religious followers. It has therefore remained in use as a monastery for more than 1,500 years.

Why the name Mor Zafaran? Because of the abundance of the crocus flower (saffron) which grows locally, and we all remarked on the gentle scent in the air around us: a sweet honey-like fragrance. Legend has it that the saffron plant was used in the mortar of the structure of the monastery, giving the stone of the building a soft amber hue.

The four of us entered the monastery with Murad and we were met by a guide from within – a soft-spoken young man of fine bearing and friendly manner.

He showed us around the important historical areas of the monastery, including the various chapels and an intriguing section underground; the basement area with a low ceiling which was apparently used by the sun worshippers of long ago. I stood there for a moment, oblivious to what our young guide was saying and was transported back to a time circa 4,000 years ago that I might have been standing on the exact spot where a man or woman uttered their prayers to Shamash, imploring the good offices of the sun god.

Our tour continued through the monastery at a gentle pace and I think we all savoured the peaceful atmosphere that prevailed throughout. Like Mor Gabriel, the fabric of this monastery was also in excellent condition and displayed how painstakingly the entire building complex has been maintained over the years. We passed through areas given over to the original divine purpose of this monastery, such as an inner courtyard in a delightful cloistered setting with olive and myrtle trees present. In another section, there was an understated fountain with a salutary message linked to the religious ethos of this place that we start out in life and can select a path that may take us on a journey of spiritual growth, but before we reach that hallowed stage of divine insight we must pass though many trials and tribulations as exemplified by the maze-like layout of the fountain which eventually leads to a central area at the heart of this labyrinth: enlightenment.

We were also able to see a Victorian printing press that came from England and was used to produce the Syriac Orthodox Bible. We were informed a copy of this holy book was despatched to Queen Victoria by way of gratitude for the gift of the printing equipment. Also on display was a rather weather-beaten sedan chair that would have been used a century previously to carry the patriarch around his parish and, of a more macabre nature, we were shown the skulls of numerous monks and bishops interred in the monastery. Our guide also told us that there are 365 rooms in Mor Zafaran – one for every day of the year, except of course a leap year if you wish to be pedantic. Another distinction associated with this monastery was that it served as the seat of the metropolitan (archbishop) of the Syriac Orthodox religion for over 600 years until 1932.

We thanked our guide for the tour and as we strolled to our vehicle, we passed by a tree-lined avenue of sugar pines as in Mor Gabriel. I was reminded of something a Jesuit priest said to me many years ago back in the Emerald Isle, that the design of churches and monasteries has a number of underlying purposes in mind and that one of them is to inculcate in the believer a sense of humility. I have to admit, therefore, to being humbled following our time spent, albeit brief, at these two monasteries, Mor Gabriel and Mor Zafaran.

> *inner peace*
> *insight*
> *a gift*
> *to share*
> *with kindness*

Our next port of call was the Kasimia Madrasa.

⚜ Kasimia Madrasa

On the outskirts of Mardin, near a large sign declaring the name of this city, Murad suggested a short walk to the madrasa, so we got out and strolled along the road until we came upon a high-walled structure which was where we were headed.

We mounted a flight of steps, entering through an impressive arch which was more than 20 m (30 ft) in height and our guide led us through a passageway into an open courtyard with a beautiful fountain without artifice, laid out according to Islamic tradition and infused with symbolism.

Here, I'm going to quote from an addendum to page 36 of my notes following our visit to this madrasa:

As Murad explained the layout of this fountain to us, I remember thinking that the design is so simple and so apt in representing how life's journey unfolds during the years and decades we live through – if we are fortunate enough to survive through to our (biblical) three score and ten. And then I thought where I would place myself in that fountain: towards the end no doubt due to my physical age of 64 [back in May 2019] but deep inside my soul I instinctively felt as if I'm still at the start of the fountain, still young and waiting to grow up as it were. I'm hungry for life and full of energy.

Here in the madrasa, as seen in the monastery, the fountain of life is symbolic of birth, life and death. In the Kasimia courtyard, the source of the water is from a wall which drains into a pool area symbolising the early part of one's existence on earth. Then the water passes through a narrow slit, signifying problems faced during the course of one's lifetime, such as a major setback, an illness or bereavement.

We were given to understand that on the Day of Judgement, every Muslim must cross the Sirat Bridge (*As-Sirat*) to enter the afterlife. Described as sharper than a sword and thinner than a strand of hair, this bridge spans the depths of hell. According to Islamic belief, the crossing of the Sirat Bridge is determined by one's deeds and faith, with those of strong faith and good deeds passing swiftly into paradise.

Also, the space inside this madrasa, the aura of serenity and all of Mesopotamia surrounding us reminded me for some reason of those memorable trips out into the desert when we lived in Saudi Arabia. I came to love the desert as a kind of second home where I could always seek out an inner peace when alone in this vast cosmos of grains of sand underfoot, which came to represent for me and within me being part of the comforting presence of countless stars above and around me in the infinite heavens stretching way, way beyond my imagination.

The Kasimia Madrasa dates from the 15th century and has been used as a mosque and as a madrasa (school) where the Islamic religion was taught. In addition, it served as a place of learning for many years where astronomy was also part of the curriculum: the pool in the open courtyard was used as a means of studying the night sky with the perfect reflection of the constellations in the smooth surface of the water.

At the back of the courtyard, there are a number of small classrooms whose doors are narrow and low. The purpose of this low entrance is to ensure the young students would bow in a reverent manner to their teachers as they entered.

To demonstrate the excellent acoustics of this madrasa which the original designers of this edifice understood 600 years ago, in a quiet voice Murad recited the opening words of the *azan*, the Muslim call to prayer, and standing on the far side of this large internal space within the building, the four of us could clearly hear the echo of his voice.

We learnt that this holy place of Islam, the Kasimia Madrasa and also the Christian monasteries of Mor Gabriel and Mor Zafaran, suffered at the hands of the fearsome Mongol ruler, Temurlane, who reigned in the 14th and 15th centuries CE when he invaded this part of the world with his marauding armies. In addition to carving out a vast empire, which at its largest extent in 1405 (the year of Temurlane's death) stretched from Sivas in the west (now in modern Türkiye) to Delhi in the east (now in modern India) and as far north as Tbilisi (modern Georgia) and Otrar (modern Kazakstan) and as far south as Hormuz (modern Iran). The territory under Mongol control was equal in size to just under half the land area of the United States today.

Visiting these three holy places, Mor Gabriel, Mor Zafaran and the Kasimia Madrasa was both a humbling and calming experience.

Back on our minibus en route to Mardin, there was the usual banter which made for some lively exchanges as we sped through this part of Mesopotamia. Suat, whose deep interest in gastronomy is recognised by all of us, or in other words, a 'foodie' as we irreverently proclaimed, teased us with his knowledge of the delicious local cuisine that awaited us.

At about 6.30pm, we arrived in Mardin and checked into our hotel, the Ninova in the old part of town. Feray had chosen well, as it was in an ideal location for a walking tour of the place which we embarked upon after a brief period to freshen up. The early evening saw us on an exploratory wander through narrow, cobbled streets and alleyways to get a feel of this city and then we headed to a local restaurant of some repute, Cercis Murat Konagi, which was highly recommended by Feray's cousin, Çiğdem. It did not disappoint. Converted from a 19th-century residential mansion and former museum, this restaurant has aesthetically retained a sense of stylish grandeur while also having a welcoming atmosphere for diners. We had an appetising dinner with excellent service to boot and we were blessed with a commanding view, we were informed, of the Mesopotamian Plain. A certain degree of celebrity status is attached to this illustrious eatery as the British monarch, King Charles III, had been there in 2004 (when Prince Charles) and we saw some photos in the foyer which commemorated his royal visitation, while also celebrating that this place is run by the well-known chef Ebru Baybara Demir, who has put her fine culinary stamp on this famous restaurant.

Our hotel was within easy walking distance and, on our return, a nightcap was suggested, except that being Ramadan the hotel was not serving alcohol. Being members of the inventive and contrary set, we devised a cunning plan to enjoy the remainder of the evening while not offending local sensibilities. Like naughty kids, we concealed our bottle of wine in a bag, helped ourselves to coffee cups from a nearby serving table and as we sat on the terrace giggling, we imbibed the forbidden fluid. From our vantage point which overlooked this part of Mardin devoid of vehicular traffic, we savoured the balmy evening, scented with local jasmine and we watched this unique part of the world amble by.

Our late-night mischievous drinking session over, Day 6 was now at an end and we, the Northern Mesopotamian quartet, retired.

*Greek-speaking (Roman)
Although Roman military personnel, government bureaucrats, the professional classes and literary figures were fluent in Latin, it was common practice for these Romans to use Greek as their lingua franca and to write using the Greek script.

*Erratic
A rock or piece of a rock transported during the Ice Age and deposited on underlying bedrock that is different.

*Glacial lake
As part of a student field trip in 1974, along with our natural sciences class, I was at the Devil's Punchbowl (a glacial lake) near Mangerton Mountain, Co. Kerry, which is not far from Killarney. The lake was silky smooth and shiny grey, and the whole place was eerily silent with a unique splendour to it which I've never forgotten.

*Pre-Cambrian rock formations
Geologically, the Pre-Cambrian epoch is the oldest part of Earth's history and the longest era, ranging in age from 4+ billion up to 570 million years ago, i.e. lasting for approximately 3.4 million years. The word 'Cambrian' comes from the Latin name for Wales, Cambria, and it is interesting to note more than 80 per cent of the rock surface of the Earth dates from this ancient epoch.

*Carboniferous

This geological epoch followed the Devonian 360 million years ago and lasted for 60 million years before being succeeded by the Permian. Limestone, sandstone and shale are common examples of rock from this era and much of the bedrock of the central plain of the island of Ireland dates from the Carboniferous, when the country was submerged beneath a warm, tropical sea.

*Karst

A form of limestone (a sedimentary rock) with a characteristic flattened surface separated by dykes (gaps in the rock) as seen in the Burren region of Co. Clare, Connemara, west of Ireland.

*Late antiquity

This spans an era of several hundred years from the 3rd–7th century CE, a transitional period marking the close of classical antiquity which in turn led to the start of the Middle Ages.

Ruins of the ancient city of Dara, Mardin Province. Dara was an eastern outpost of the Roman Empire during the Byzantine Era.

Ruined main street – known as Palace Street – ancient city of Dara, aka Anastasiopolis.

Sarcophagi, Dara.

Former church and ossuary etched out of the rock, Dara.

Close-up of the ruins in the ancient city of Dara, also known as Anastasiopolis, Mardin Province.

Yazidi artwork – peacock signifying immortality.

Entrance to the Zindan Cistern was through the basement of this house in the village of Oğuz, Mardin Province, near the ancient city of Dara.

Floodlit Zindan Cistern.

Entrance to the oldest Syriac Orthodox monastery in the world, Mor Gabriel, founded in 397 CE.

Interior of Mor Gabriel Monastery.

Two bell towers of Mor Gabriel Monastery.

Inner courtyard, Mor Gabriel; Syriac script on archway.

Copy of the Last Supper artwork, Mor Gabriel Monastery.

Postcard of Mor Zafaran Monastery.

Mor Zafaran Monastery.

Entrance to the Kasimia Madrasa, Mardin.

Path of life fountain and pool, Mor Zafaran Monastery, echoed in the Kasimia Madrasa.

Inner courtyard, Mor Zafaran Monastery.

City of Mardin, where people have lived for more than 6,000 years.

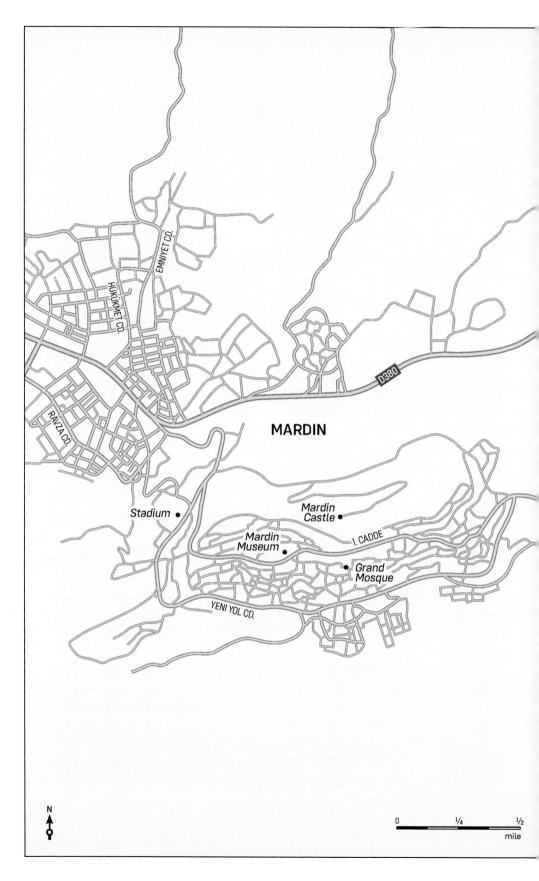

MARDIN

EMNİYET CD.

HÜKÜMET CD.

RANZA CD.

D380

Stadium •

Mardin
Castle •

Mardin
Museum •

1. CADDE

• Grand
Mosque

YENİ YOL CD.

N

0   ¼   ½
                mile

DAY 7

WEDNESDAY 29TH MAY 2019

*Discovering a hilltop city with ancient origins at
the heart of iconic Northern Mesopotamia*

*when embracing
the enchantment of times past,
let the vibe
of Mesopotamia
draw you closer*

PROPOSED ITINERARY:
▷ Walking tour of Mardin, the Grand Mosque and the Mardin Museum
▷ Fast food par excellence with the best pide in town and a café where culture rules
▷ Evening – dinner at a rooftop restaurant with a view of the Mesopotamian Plain
▷ Exploring Mardin at night

We were grateful that we were going to be able to spend two consecutive nights in Mardin, which meant less wear and tear on our creaking bones. A word about our hotel, the Ninova: located near the base of the hill adorned by the imposing Mardin Castle, everything about the place was attractive and comfortable, plus the staff and the service we received were all excellent. The room was a decent size if a tad over-decorated but we had great views from our window – especially of the Mesopotamian Plain stretching as far as the eye could see. The other advantage of this hotel was that it was within easy walking distance of the various places we were due to see while staying in Mardin.

Murad proposed the Grand Mosque of Mardin, which turned out to be well worth seeing. Dating from the 11th century where historical records suggest it may have been constructed on the footings of a former church, this distinctive place of worship possessed two minarets when first built by the Seljuks, but one of them collapsed many centuries ago. In keeping with all great edifices dedicated to the glorification of God, be they synagogues, temples, gurdwaras, churches, mosques and so on, this place of worship definitely made its mark while exuding a peaceful splendour endowed with holiness.

Mardin market now attracted our interest, with many open-air stalls selling all manner of wares crammed into the narrow alleyways and streets. As we strolled through this extensive outdoor bazaar, I was charmed by many of the stallholders greeting us warmly while inviting us to view their merchandise. But what fascinated me was being able to see the tailor, for instance, surrounded by different cuts of material, beavering away on his machinery sewing an item of clothing; the cobbler with different pieces of leather about him fashioning a new pair of shoes; and thanks to the availability of precious metals since ancient times, one observed coppersmiths, silversmiths and goldsmiths painstakingly toiling away, producing jewellery, coffee and tea utensils, salt and pepper sets, trays and other pieces, carving out patterns of a classical nature drawn from a rich Ottoman and Islamic inventory. I saw many jewellers, themselves working in earnest concentration on some fine pieces with the assistance of a large magnifying glass. In addition, we came across shops selling a tremendous variety of spices and nuts, including walnuts, pistachios and lokum (Turkish delight), while other vendors were engaged in the selling of perfumes and fragrances, together with rosewater and bergamot – on passing these latter establishments, we were invariably offered samples to try.

This experience of the busy Mardin market with a welcoming atmosphere prevailing left a deep impression while also giving me a glimpse of what it might have been like travelling along the Silk Road some years past.

There was one antique shop we came across that was a veritable Aladdin's Cave selling all manner of objects, bric-a-brac and artwork but it became obvious that it specialised in something quite unusual and stunning to look at: *tuğras*. These are the ornate and highly stylised calligraphic monograms or individual seals of the rulers down through the centuries, used when official documents were being drawn up.

Each Ottoman leader had his very own *tuğra*, i.e. the signature of the sultan, and it is a joy to marvel at the intricate interwoven detail that is conveying so much in terms of the political, spiritual, artistic and personal. Historically, the *tuğra* became an established custom in the 13th century with Sultan Orhan I, whereby the incoming sultan sought to stamp his political and spiritual authority right from the very start of the reign. A court scribe would be selected to design the new and unique seal of the newly anointed sultan in accordance with a traditional template, with an in-built flexibility where individual flourishes pertaining to the new ruler were incorporated. This royal cipher would then find application on official documents, coinage and even on furniture and crockery used by or associated with the sultan. This practice of putting the stamp of the head of state on many aspects of daily life became firmly established within the Ottoman psyche and remained in use for the next 600 years, reaching its peak in terms of inventive embellishment during the reign of Suleyman the Magnificent in the 16th century.[24] It is a motif that survives to this day in many different ways, often to be seen emblazoned on urban

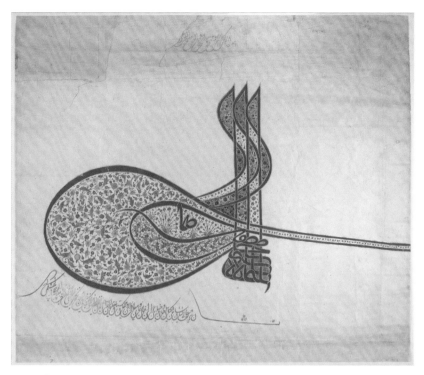

Tuğra of Ottoman ruler, Suleyman the Magnificent, 1520–1566 CE

buildings, on posters and even in contemporary Turkish advertising.

I came across so many references on the topic of *tuğras* that I joked with my wife that one could write a book on this very subject, such is the history, detail, cultural reference points and visual content of these unique seals of leadership from a bygone age which portrayed a remarkable aesthetic balance of the prescribed and what could be freely expressed.

Located not far from the River Tigris dating back to the Bronze Age, Mardin was once part of the Hurrian Empire which reigned supreme some 4,000 years ago. This city was a major terminus on the Silk Road of old which, in a long-gone era during the time of the Hittites, was called Azala and then Marida (meaning 'fortress' in Syriac) when the Romans were present. As we came to understand from the many places seen on this excursion, Mardin is no exception to experiencing much in the way of influences from history, religion, politics, art and philosophy over the millennia, and in terms of a contemporary picture, the population is just under 90,000 people with Turkish and Arabic roots.

The one topographical aspect that dominates this city is the high hill that overlooks Mardin and is the result of very ancient geological forces involving plate tectonics where the (continuing) collision between the African and European plates has resulted, among other things, in this mountainous formation. On top of this hilly outcrop is Mardin Castle, first constructed 3,000 years ago by the Mitanni during the Hurrian epoch, rebuilt and enlarged under Roman rule and again reworked in the 10th century CE during the Hamdani period. This city and its surroundings are chock full of history, I came to understand.

Blessed with unbroken good weather as we continued with our walking tour of Mardin, we came to realise that the design of this city still followed a medieval town plan with some narrow streets and very old-looking buildings in a good state of repair, which we figured could be 400 years or more in vintage. Striking religious symbolism with a unifying theme was also apparent on the wall of a hotel we came across (not the Ninova) where we spotted imagery holy to the four faiths of Judaism, Islam, Christianity and Yazidism (see page 203).

As we walked, I noted variations on a theme of how an idiosyncratic multicoloured picture was displayed in many shops and stalls. This was of a woman (ornately made-up and well dressed) while also in possession of a tail of a snake or serpent. In one case, I saw a framed painting of this female human-cum-animal character on the wall of a clothes shop; on spotting me, the proprietor welcomed me in to take a photo.

Depictions of the mythological figure of Shahmaran – half-woman, half-serpent. The photo on the right shows a Mardin shopkeeper holding a scarf emblazoned with a striking likeness of Shahmaran.

On inquiry, I was informed that this was a famous figure from Persian mythology called *Shahmaran* – a mythical creature which was half-woman, half-snake. In ancient Persian folklore, her name means Queen of the Snakes and she is very much part of the culture of this region involving a love story between two people, Shahmaran and Camasb, who lived together in a cave. Later, the unfortunate Shahmaran came to a sticky end when betrayed by her lover, Camasb.

Lunch was had from the Ebrar Mahalli Yemekler Restaurant, with a reputation for serving the best pide* and lahmaçun* in town. We took our carefully wrapped takeaways to a local garden and devoured them. As I write these words, the memory of the enticing flavour of this food is making me hungry.

We continued our walking tour and viewed examples of philanthropic works in the form of houses and various buildings undertaken by former Mardin residents in previous centuries who set money aside for the construction of housing, schools and other places for impoverished members of the community. On our wander, we came across a bistro of character, the Kultur Café, that took our immediate fancy due to its funky design, welcoming atmosphere, bookshelves populated with interesting volumes that we did peruse and cool Turkish music playing in the background. It's one of those things when you enter a place for the first time, the ambience hits you and, in this case, it drew us in with a cosy embrace and we all remarked that it felt 'just right'. The four of us were quite content to be sitting there in the Kultur Café, enjoying our coffee and a piece of cake while listening to a beautiful piece of music, 'Yola Çiktim Mardine' ('I hit the road, Mardin'), sung by local musician, Berdan Mardini, which is a Mardin folk song echoing the unique sound of the region's rich culture that fell pleasantly on our ears. And all this because we happened upon a delightful watering hole in Mardin, a city where many languages are spoken, such as Turkish, Kurdish, Arabic and Syriac.

Next on our list was the Mardin Museum, which when compared to others we had recently been to is relatively small, but nevertheless well laid-out where a sense of the aesthetic has been taken into consideration. The imposing entrance was very much a leading-edge affair with the foyer encased in green-tinted glass on three sides. An important facet of this museum which one felt the curators were at pains to highlight was that Mardin acted as a crucible of different cultures, peoples and faiths who have lived within this city over many centuries and from the displays within the section called 'People of Mardin', one came to learn that Jews, Christians and Muslims have co-existed in this area for millennia. There was a tangible air of inclusivity from this part of the museum, including a section entitled 'The Spread of Christianity in Mardin'.

In addition, this museum had its own 'take' on the many archaeological eras and what specimens of interest from key periods of the past to highlight from the year dot up to the 21st century, and I appreciated how this arc of time and complexity of vision had been presented thus, making it easy to grasp the variety of detail within this exhibition of rich local history. Again, I was deeply appreciative of the brief and legible details in both Turkish and English which spanned nearly 20,000 years, starting with the Palaeolithic (Stone Age) of 15,000 BCE up to present-day Türkiye.

Of particular note was a picture of the Stele of Naramsin from the Akkadian period of nearly 4,250 years ago. A stele, as you will recall, is a monument made of wood, metal or stone and is usually erected in the ground as a memorial of some important historic event, such as a military battle. In this case, the Stele of Naramsin is a commemorative carving in a piece of limestone 200 cm (79 in) in height and up to 150 cm (59 in) in width; the original is currently on display at the Louvre in Paris, France. The victory memorialised is that of a struggle of King Naramsin over the Lullubi people from the Zagros mountains (in present day Iran) and contains a visual relief of the battle while also showing some cuneiform inscriptions in Akkadian and Elamite text. Such a stele would have performed a useful public relations exercise on the part of the ruler, as the educated elite – usually less than 1 per cent of the population – would have been satisfied with a written message inscribed in cuneiform whereas the other 99 per cent of unlettered people would have instead grasped the graphical meaning of the display. This stele from ancient times, therefore, was a cleverly executed piece of official 'artspeak' which had true mass appeal and could be understood by people from all walks of life.

This part of Northern Mesopotamia has attracted interest from many travellers over the years. The Venetian explorer Marco Polo was in Mardin in the 1270s on his extensive travels from Venice through Mesopotamia and onwards to China. After a period of 24 years, he returned home. The story is he was accused of commanding a Venetian ship in a war against Genoa and was captured by the Genovese authorities and put in prison for three years. While languishing in gaol, he entertained his fellow prisoners and guards with tales of his travels throughout Asia and a cellmate, Rustichello da Pisa, committed these stories to paper in 1298. This famous travelogue was entitled *The Description of the World*, but became better known as *The Travels*. Just over half a century later, Mardin was also visited, in 1327, by the acclaimed Berber explorer Ibn Battuta from Morocco who was en route to performing *Hajj** for the first time. Ibn Battuta, however, covered far more territory than his Venetian counterpart, encompassing north, east and west central Africa; Mesopotamia; the Arabian peninsula and a swathe of Asian territory stretching all the way from present-day Iraq to China, including Vietnam, Indonesia, Sri Lanka, the Maldives and Oman. Ibn Battuta recorded his vast journeyings over 30 years in a book called *A Masterpiece to Those Who Contemplate the Wonders of Cities and the Marvels of Travelling*; it too came to be known by the catchier title of *The Travels*, thus sharing commonality with Marco Polo in the name of their respective publications.

> *Travelling – it gives you home in thousands strange places (sic), then leaves you a stranger in your own land.*
> Ibn Battuta

Marco Polo is an historical individual well-known to me from schooldays back in Ireland and was something of a hero from an exploration point of view. As it happens, Ibn Battuta is also a familiar figure as I had come to learn about this larger-than-life 14th century personage while living in Jeddah, Saudi Arabia during the early 1980s. I had the good fortune to work for the English language section of Radio Jeddah, part of the Saudi Broadcasting Service, where I was given the role of presenting on air about famous figures in the Arab world, including Ibn Battuta.

My boss at the radio station, Yusuf, was a Palestinian who had recently completed a PhD in Anglo-Irish literature. Our conversations were enlightening; I learned so much from him about Irish literature, his views on Yeats and Joyce, the stream of consciousness, and the influence of Irish writing on Arab literature. These discussions left an indelible impression on me.

Our exploration of Mardin over, we returned to our hotel to get ready for dinner. Once dickeyed up in our best bib and tucker for the evening, a short walk took us to the Seyr-I Mardin Restaurant with an excellent reputation not only for its cuisine of a local flavour, but also its rooftop setting which has a commanding, and I do mean commanding, view of the Mesopotamian Plain stretching as far and wide as the eye can see.

We got there shortly before sunset and fortunately with a table booked, as the place was already nearly full and we were informed by the waiting staff that being Ramadan, they would only serve us drinks and food post-sundown. This suited us fine as we made ourselves comfortable in this amazing location.

The *Maghrib* (sunset) call to prayer (*adhan*) sounded out from the nearby Grand Mosque which meant that fasting was now at an end.

Dinner consisted of a Ramadan platter which was a mélange of Mardin traditional dishes served with the Ramazan pidesi – a flat, round bread made of wheat flour topped with sesame seeds and having a weave-like patterned crust. As we were finishing off our meal, the light began to fade when the sun dipped beneath the horizon. Looking north from our table was the outline of the hills on top of which sits Mardin Castle and to the south, the everlasting sweeping views of the Mesopotamian Plain extending from where we were in southern Türkiye and on to modern-day Syria and Iraq. It was a marvellous moment to see Mardin Castle change from being an outline against the darkening sky to being dramatically floodlit as night fell. Just about every diner there appeared as mesmerised as we were, snapping away with their phones and cameras to catch that moment. As I focused my lens on the single surviving minaret of the Grand Mosque which soared above Mardin, a swift flew into view. That split second of wonder was captured and preserved on film.

Afterwards, we wandered through town and came across a bar where music and song were in full flow. We managed to get the last free table and enjoyed a great time as a hip-looking duet of a guy and a gal (as they'd say in 'saaf' London) wowed their audience with some jazzy and smoochie numbers. It was well worth the visit and the place we'd come across by chance had a great atmosphere to it. It was an evening of pure joy for the quartet to join in the prevailing mood and singing along with the young crowd there.

It now being the small hours, we strolled back to the Ninova and we savoured it to the last, knowing that we'd be departing from Mardin in the morning after breakfast. One notable sight we came across just before we reached our hotel was a solitary donkey standing on the pavement decked out in incredibly colourful regalia, with lots of bells and decorative motifs on show, so this had to be documented in a photograph. Before I leave the romance of this priceless evening behind us, I'd like to record at the end of Day 7 on our truly memorable journey that I feel exceptionally fortunate to be able to complete such a trip, that all four of us together are close friends for longer than we can remember, with Feray and Suat married for the past 34 years, Rashida and myself married for 42 years (and all still on speaking terms!), thankfully in good health and in a position to be able to enjoy such an experience in this wonderful part of south-eastern Türkiye in what was ancient Northern Mesopotamia.

Later on, following our excursion, the whole world was plunged into an existential struggle for survival on account of the lethal Covid-19 virus pandemic which still hovers ominously over the world, not to mention other threats that always appear out of the woodwork with alarming regularity. We should doubly cherish, therefore, the happy and uplifting memory of our journey. Let this book be a celebration of that unique and invaluable time in our lives, when we spent the most wonderful eight days in each other's company relishing every moment in this part of the world. Our journey in history, through history and about history will no doubt continue.

With that, we were back in our rooms and the world of pragmatic existence with some hasty packing – in reality, chucking things in our respective suitcases to be ready for the morning's 9am get-away after breakfast.

We slept soundly.

---

*Pide
A Turkish flatbread, oval in shape, with toppings such as ground meat and onion, cheese and spinach or cheese and suçuk (Turkish spicy sausage), and usually served with a shepherd salad consisting of shredded lettuce, tomatoes, cucumbers, mint and other herbs with a generous squeeze of lemon on top.

*Lahmaçun
Think of it as a super-thin Turkish pizza with a blend of spices, minced meat and fresh vegetables such as tomatoes, peppers and herbs. It is usually round in shape and can be rolled up like a pancake.
Both pide and lahmaçun are the perfect take-away foods and go well with ayran, a plain yogurt drink.

*Hajj
A religious pilgrimage to Makkah, Saudi Arabia, performed by Muslims as one of the five pillars of Islam.

Street scene, Mardin.

Mardin Castle at the summit of the hill overlooking the city.

Elevated scene showing the Mesopotamian Plain in the distance, Mardin.

Doorway, Mardin.

Religious symbolism in Mardin – Yazidi, Judaism, Christianity and Islam.

Grand Mosque with its one surviving minaret, Mardin.

Scene just outside the Grand Mosque.

Shadirvan in the courtyard of the Grand Mosque – a source of water for drinking and ritual ablutions.

Street scene, Mardin.

Silversmith at work.

Just in case you need to find your bearings
– Mardin street sign.

Street vendor, Mardin.

Mardin Museum.

People of Mardin exhibit, Mardin Museum.

Masonry exhibit, Mardin Museum.

Grand Mosque at sunset with the Mesopotamian Plain in the distance.

Grand Mosque at night.

Night in Mardin.

Dressed to kill in Mardin.

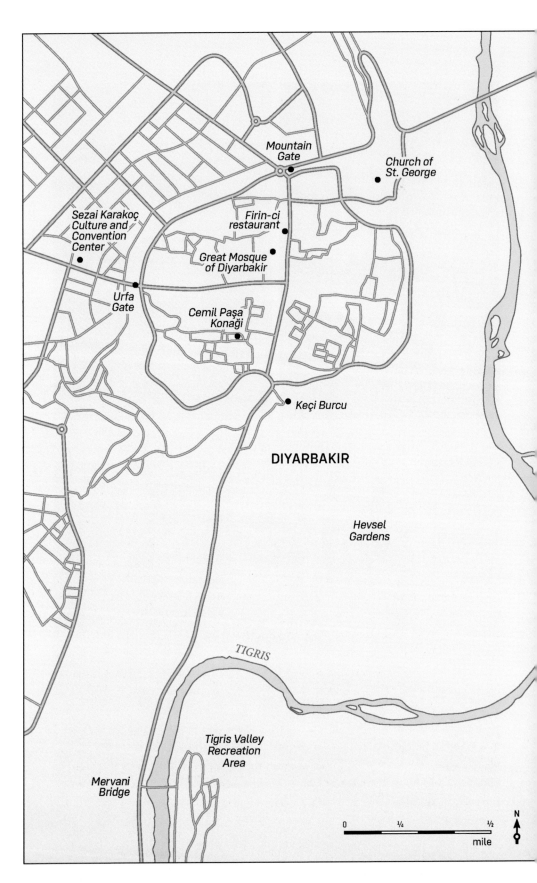

DAY 8

◁

THURSDAY 30ᵀᴴ MAY 2019

The Grand Finale: the delight
of Diyarbakir and the River Tigris

Diyarbakir in all its glory
Kurdish crucible,
by the hallowed River Tigris
like a beacon of light
illuminating time's divinity

PROPOSED ITINERARY:
▷ Depart Mardin and onwards to the city of Diyarbakir
▷ Mervani Bridge and Diyarbakir city walls
▷ Lunch in Firin-ci restaurant, a former hamam
▷ Check into Hotel Divan and a remarkable encounter
▷ With great regret, say thank you and goodbye to that amazing duo, Murad,
  our tour guide and Halil, our driver
▷ Evening in Diyarbakir

After an early start, we departed the Ninova Hotel at 9am, leaving Mardin behind us we drove up the main highway, the D-950 and an hour and 20 minutes later arrived at our first destination of the day, an iconic landmark just outside Diyarbakir. Straddling the River Tigris is an ancient bridge called, we were informed, the following: the Dicle Bridge, the Ten-Arches Bridge, the Sylvan Bridge and the Mervani Bridge. This must be the only bridge I know of which possesses four names! The Mervani name stems from the Mervani people, who were part of this region which has strong Kurdish origins; Dicle is the Turkish for Tigris and Sylvan because the bridge leads on to the nearby town of Sylvan, which figures large in Kurdish history and culture.

The first bridge had been erected by the Romans and the current structure is a magnificent example of design from the Marwanid Era* when it was constructed of black volcanic basalt in 1065. The solid brickwork of this ten-arched bridge replaced previous versions of this crossing point over the River Tigris just 3 km (2 miles) south of Diyarbakir and is, therefore, more than 950 years old.

No vehicular traffic uses this bridge now and thoughtfully the local authority constructed a more modern version just over a kilometre away to ensure contemporary transportation needs continued to be met, while not detracting from the beauty of this ancient example of engineering excellence spanning this major river.

We walked onto the bridge and I gazed in wonder at the River Tigris flowing beneath us. Looking at this view conjured up a special moment in me. Here was another waterway of historic proportions instilled in my mind since early childhood. How many geography, history and religious instruction classes of old, back in Ireland in the 1960s and early 70s, had I sat through where distant foreign places, peoples and rivers, such as Antioch, Tarsus, Sumerian, Persian, Euphrates, Mesopotamia and Tigris had been voiced and these seeds of divine magic had been planted in my young brain awaiting fulfilment all through my life. Now I was mentally pinching myself in the same way as when I had looked upon the River Euphrates four days previously. Such happenings imprint themselves deeply on the psyche – especially at the age of 65+ – as you get the inkling you are completing a vast arc of learning set in motion like an arrow shot from a bow more than a half a century ago in one's youth. All was new, being laid down on that Petri dish of a young brain learnt not only from direct experience but also from books, magazines, teachers, parents, older relatives, films, radio or television. Then one's life flashes by and fortunately an opportunity arises in one's seventh decade of life to be able to visit these wondrous places that seemed so remote in the past. I also thought of those I had known over the years, no longer around, who were unable to share this experience.

It was a very moving and humbling moment as I stood on the Mervani Bridge, peering down at the smooth-running water of the Tigris. For some reason I was reminded of Marcus Aurelius and his thoughts on time and his version of *carpe diem* – i.e. grabbing that fleeting element of passing existence: "give yourself a gift – the present moment" which this former Roman general, emperor and writer had described in his *Meditations*. I realised I was doing just that, enjoying the entire experience of this present moment, knowing my darling wife whom I could never live without was next to me, as were two very dear friends of longstanding nearby. I thought of our two sons back home in England; that the morning around me was singularly beautiful as the sun shone in a cloudless blue sky; that my inner being was additionally comforted by the sounds of the music of nature as I could hear the river gushing by through the arches of this solid bridge which has stood for nearly a thousand years.

I looked up from the River Tigris and, in the distance on elevated ground, I could make out the old city walls of Diyarbakir.

oh footsteps, footsteps
should i follow thee?
in my dreams
how will i ever know
the way, the truth, the life
can reach those far-off horizons?
in the morning
clearflowing energies
of hope may fade
but the longing always remains
always

My daydreams paused when one of our group expressed a wish to have a coffee by the Tigris and even though it was Ramadan, Murad managed to find the perfect sheltered spot in a café near the water's edge where we continued to enjoy the view of this Mesopotamian river of old. We sat for a while in this haven of calm with the waters of this great river just next to us with barely another soul nearby. Such moments of peacefulness were to be treasured and will become future remembrances that will be a delight to revisit *ad infinitum*.

Diyarbakir – in all its glory

> In spring, when the flood period of the Tigris has passed and its limpid water
> begins to flow again in a stable current, all Diyarbakir's inhabitants, rich and poor
> alike, move with their entire families to the bank of the Tigris. They set up camp
> with their tents and pavilions along this wide water, on plots they have inherited …
> and cultivate their gardens with fruit, vegetables and flowers. They cultivate here a
> special type of basil … in a month's time it becomes thick as a forest and tall as a
> spear, impenetrable to the glance.

Evliya Çelebi, *Seyahatname* [*Book of Travels*], 1641–65
Further references to Evliya Çelebi can be seen on Days 1, 3 and 5.

We set off for our final stopping off point: Diyarbakir. The name of this ancient city, which has its origins going back to the Stone Age, possesses an interesting history as the place was once called Ameda, and when the Romans appeared on the scene, they called it something similar, Amida. The Kurdish name is Amed and its official Turkish name, Diyarbakir, means 'land of copper', as this alludes to the copper deposits in the vicinity. Let's not forget the Arabs, who also were historic players in occupying this place, and the Bakr tribe was instrumental in holding the reins of power here at one stage so that in Arabic, Diyarbakir means 'land of the tribe of Bakr'. Then, you had all the various empires and groups of people who set foot in this part of Mesopotamia and held Diyarbakir and its hinterland in their grasp for a wee while: we've come across them before, such as the Hurrians, Arameans, Assyrians, Urartu, Armenians, Achaemenids, Persians, Medians, Seleucids and Parthians with the Romans soon after.

We learnt the city walls were first constructed some 5,000 years ago and then rebuilt by the Romans when they were in the city. They are made of black volcanic basalt and encircle Diyarbakir completely, being largely intact to this day. The early medieval redesign of the walls completed during the onset of the Islamic era has remained unchanged with four gates and a large number of watchtowers still in existence. It is worth noting that Diyarbakir has always occupied a strategic location by the River Tigris, close to fertile land and also endowed with valuable natural resources such as copper, silver and gold. More recently, petroleum has been discovered in the area around the city of Batman about 120 miles north-east of Midyat, where we'd been two days previously.

We had entered Diyarbakir through the Urfa Gate and then made our way through part of the city over to the Mardin Gate. There, with no handrails or safety barriers evident, we gingerly ascended the steep steps to reach the top of the city wall. It took us a moment or two to get our bearings, especially as there was a sheer drop of some 10 m (33 ft) on either side of the flattened top of the fortification about 4 m (13½ ft) wide. From this vantage point, we had a commanding view of the solid-looking perimeter wall protecting a city of one and three quarter million people: it is one of the largest Kurdish-population cities in Türkiye. Looking in a south-easterly direction back to where we'd just come from, the Mervani Bridge was easily visible in the middle distance.

With repeated caution, we descended from the city walls and while crossing a busy road spotted something of interest. At first glance, it appeared to be a slightly unusual traffic island in the middle of a bustling thoroughfare, but this square-shaped building with alternating layers of dark and light colouration on its exterior topped off with a pyramid-style roof is in fact a sultan's tomb. On looking up the history, it turns out it is the mausoleum of Sultan Şuca Türbesi who lived in the 13th century, a prince who ruled Diyarbakir, and this historic building is an example of the Seljuk style of architecture built not long after his death in 1237. On closer inspection, one could see that this resting place was covered in turquoise-tinted tiles and the exterior is adorned with elaborate geometric patterns and calligraphy. It is an important pilgrimage site for Muslims in the region.

On foot, we made our way to the Cemil Paşa Konaği (Cemil Pasha Mansion) on Ali Pasha Street, a large city property built in the 1880s by an Ottoman official who had been in charge of Yemen at the tail end of the Arabian peninsula. In this area we also came across a remnant from the past next to the perimeter wall of a mosque nearby at the foot of a minaret: the lonely remains of Roman columns.

En route we passed the houses of two famous Turkish/Kurdish writers and popped in to see the former abode of one of them, Jahid Siteharanji, who wrote: "At 35, I'm at the age when my father died."

This mixed-heritage architectural feature using Roman and Islamic building materials and styles was repeated a little later on, but for the time being we entered the Cemil Pasha Mansion and were able to wander around the inner garden graced with an attractive fountain and on this warm sunny day, its psychological cooling effect was most welcome. There is something very comforting about hearing the waters of a fountain as it weaves its magic spell of comfort and calm.

flowing waters
soul soothing
creating and recreating reflections
bearing our dreams
over time

Within the mansion grounds is the Diyarbakir City Museum, which was established in 2015 and designed to be an exhibition of this city and its people. Interestingly, the explanations accompanying the displays in this compact museum were in Turkish and Kurdish with no English available unfortunately. Even a glance at the imagery on show gave me to understand that the place is culturally, religiously and racially diverse. I learnt that when the museum was established, there had been a *rapprochement* between the Turkish authorities and Kurdish community leaders which facilitated the bilingual explanations of all the items on show.

The Sheikh Matar Mosque dating from 1500 CE is a house of prayer in possession of a well-known feature, as its minaret is separate from the mosque while being set on the remains of four Roman columns – hence the nickname, the four-legged minaret. As we admired this building and its unusual design, we were met by a friendly group of women. It turned out that they were offering us some coffee to taste, as they had just opened up their shop as their own business two days previously. Being greeted in such a friendly fashion and being offered a sample induced us to enter their establishment. As we bought some coffee, honey and nuts – all beautifully wrapped in their distinctive-looking packaging, I took several photos of this outgoing group of female entrepreneurs and we wished them well as we departed.

We visited the Sülüklü Han where we downed some fresh lemonade to quench our thirst. For your information, *sülüklü* means leech in Turkish and refers historically to when leeches were dispensed as medical treatments in years gone by at this *han*. Then, onwards to the Great Mosque of Diyarbakir noted for its distinctive geometric design and remarkable shadirvan, a communal fountain used for drinking and ablution, which added a unique feature within the precincts of the mosque. Built on the site of a former church and inspired by the layout of the Great Mosque of Damascus, this site has served as a place of worship for both Christians and Muslims and is a significant religious site in Islam. The mosque is known for accommodating the four different traditions of Islamic jurisprudence. Numerous carvings and Kufic inscriptions adorn the structure, and we stayed awhile to savour the essence of this historical and holy place.

Somebody then suggested lunch and we headed off to a very popular Diyarbakir restaurant, the Firin-Ci, which is actually a converted historical hamam under a dramatic domed roof, reminding us of the Grand Hamam of Istanbul we had been to several years earlier. As we were having our lunch and chatting with Murad, he told us about his family and his former life as an academic now turned tour guide – a fascinating and moving story.

Digestion complete, we were off on our next foray to see the main Diyarbakir Museum which we got to by walking through the market and what was an ancient gate in the city walls, which in turn led into a pleasant public park. A short while later, we found ourselves at the Artuqids Arch (itself an artefact from Roman times) which was the main entrance into the museum complex – a converted prison – spacious gardens, two cafés and including the roofless Christian church of St George dating from 300 CE.

The main museum itself was a stunning array of historical items and is well worth a detour. Two of the displays deserve a mention here: a 13th-century robot and obsidian. Let's take a look at this extraordinary automaton from more than 800 years ago invented by the Arabian polymath, Ismail al-Jazari,[25] or to give him his full name, Badi az-Zaman Abu I-Izz ibn Ismail ibn ar-Razaz al-Jazari, who was born in 1136 in Cizre (in present day Türkiye on the River Tigris, near the border with Syria) and lived until 1206 coming from what Arabs call *Jazira*, (meaning 'the island') but in this context, the term *Jazira* refers to Northern Mesopotamia. In addition to being an inventor and serving as chief engineer to the Sultan, al-Jazari was a pioneer in cybernetics (from the Greek κυβερνήτης, meaning the art of steering), the study of the effective control of complex systems involving the interaction of machines and living things. He was an expert in a number of other fields, including mechanical engineering, metallurgy, art and mathematics. Think of al-Jazari as an Arab equivalent of Leonardo da Vinci, except that the latter lived 300 years *after* his Mesopotamian counterpart. Al-Jazari wrote on many subjects but perhaps his most notable publication was *The Book of Knowledge of Ingenious Mechanical Devices*, which appeared in 1206, the year of his demise. In this publication he describes a large number of mechanical tools that he designed and modelled himself, including that of a self-propelled automaton powered by the use of water, i.e. a robot. The same book contains a wealth of technical illustrations with engineering as an underlying theme, various contraptions and appliances including his famous elephant clock, a design for a camshaft, gears, pumps of various kinds and even a water irrigation system. Also on display in the museum were contemporary 13th-century pictures which evidenced many of these remarkable designs in their made-out form. It is astonishing to contemplate that al-Jazari was a pioneer in many of the areas he wrote on.

Let me turn to the other item of unusual interest on show at the Diyarbakir Museum: obsidian. This is a form of volcanic glass which is usually dark in colour, being black, grey or darkish brown, with a glasslike texture and heavy to the touch. Obsidian also possesses a distinctive curved fracture appearance (called a conchoidal fracture, if interested) when it breaks or shears off.

Numerous deposits of obsidian are in this part of Northern Mesopotamia and since ancient times this mineral has enjoyed a variety of uses, such as prehistoric weapons and mirrors, blades for cutting, including surgical use in circumcision (ouch), gemstones and even the plinth for an audio turntable.

Talking about obsidian reminds me of this anecdote: about 12 years ago when Rashida was working in a nursing home in Surrey, she came home one evening with an unusual gift. It was from the son of an elderly resident who used to tell Rashida about her extensive travels during her younger days. Sadly, this elderly lady had passed away and her son, aware of the many conversations his mother and Rashida had shared, kindly gave my wife this uncommon present.

On arrival home, Rashida showed me the object in question, asking me if I knew what it was. Drawing on one's memory not yet ga-ga from misspent student days in the Trinity College geology department, I was able to pronounce it as obsidian without hesitation. My wife responded, "Smart Alec, aren't you?"

Meanwhile, as we exited from this absorbing museum in Diyarbakir, we almost bumped into what we thought was a newly married glamorous couple having their picture taken, as the bride and groom were being asked to pose in different ways for what seemed to be a very attentive professional photographer. But getting married in Ramadan is not the norm in Türkiye, plus we could see there were no guests present, except for a lot of technical people in attendance and some lighting gizmos focused on the well-dressed woman and man. So Feray and Suat inquired, and we were informed a fashion magazine was doing a photo shoot with weddings as the theme using this historic backdrop.

We continued our tour of the museum estate and gazed at the actual prison building from the outside, as it is not open to the public, then came to the roofless church of St George which is 1,700 years old, where Roman and Byzantine influences are evident.

We learnt that while the people today of Diyarbakir no longer practise the semi-nomadic lifestyle described by the Ottoman explorer Evliya Çelebi, described previously, the River Tigris continues to play an important cultural and recreational role in Diyarbakir. The river serves as a vantage point for fishing, boating and picnicking, while the waters of the Tigris support local agriculture through crop irrigation.

> *The people of Diyarbakir are the envy of the world for the delights they enjoy for seven or eight months of the year along the bank of the Tigris; when their nights are like the Night of Power (Laylat al-Qadr) and their days like the holiday of the Festival of Sacrifice (Eid al-Adha) holding concerts … and thinking to snatch a bit of pleasure from this transitory world.*

Evliya Çelebi, *Seyahatname [Book of Travels]*; 1641–65

It was now about 4ish on this Thursday, the eighth day of our excursion to Northern Mesopotamia, so tea-time beckoned, and we installed ourselves in one of the cafés in this inner castle area. Fortunately we had a marvellous, uninterrupted view of the River Tigris and surrounding area which includes, among other things, the Hevsel Gardens, added to the UNESCO World Heritage List in 2015, alongside the old city walls of Diyarbakir. We chilled and supped on something pleasant – having a cuppa and gazing at the Tigris, as you do. Murad suggested further places to visit after our break but the four of us having travelled so far and absorbed so much in the preceding week, and mindful that our tour guide hadn't seen his family in more than seven days, suggested, with a twinge of regret, to end our trip of a lifetime. It was decided, therefore, to go our different ways: that we would be dropped at our hotel, and for Murad and our driver to start their return journey home.

The journey through Northern Mesopotamia was done. Mixed feelings swirled inside me: a deep sense of accomplishment shared with my wife and dear friends, joy, relief, but there was a bittersweet longing for the adventures that now lay behind, yet a newfound anticipation for the ones that awaited me beyond the horizon. Perhaps in time, when conditions permit and harmony reigns in the region, the remainder of Mesopotamia can be explored and experienced to the full – travelling through Syria and Iraq, navigating the full length of those two great rivers of old, the Euphrates and the Tigris, and their spellbinding hinterland. A future dream to be realised, perhaps.

As we drove to the Hotel Divan, which we had booked so as to be close to the airport as we had a very early flight departing the following morning, there was a palpable air of sadness. Final thank yous and goodbyes of a profound nature were exchanged in the foyer with Murad kindly wishing us: "Have a nice life." As our tour guide walked away, I realised we had all been privileged to share time with a fellow human being who had given so much to all of us. We were all in agreement that both our driver and Murad had been excellent ambassadors for their country.

As we were checking in, a young woman and gentleman helped us with the formalities. The name of the male receptionist, though, intrigued me, as he introduced himself as Şeymous – pronounced Shaymousse – sounding very like the Irish for James, i.e. Séamus. I asked him how come he had an Irish-sounding name. And lo, he told me that his father was Irish and his mother, Turkish. And yes, he did have some interesting tales to tell. A Turkish gift of the blarney was surely in this young man's genes!

The clocks tolled the hour of six and the quartet were in need of a restorative of a strongish liquid kind, but there was a problem as the hotel bar was closed. What to do? Şeymous rose to the challenge in two shakes of a lamb's tail. Not only was the hotel bar opened for just the four of us but our new Irish-Turkish friend conjured up a snack of cheese, humus, tomatoes, olives, peanuts and other tasty titbits that was just the biscuit to accompany the excellent wines of the region he had provided. Şeymous kept us well entertained as we sipped on our drinks and nibbled on the *mezes* laid out before us.

While Şeymous waxed lyrical of his Irish-Turkish heritage, with parents originating from two nations thousands of miles apart, I was reminded of a story I had read where two Irish scribes had diligently worked in a monastery scriptorium in the north-west of Ireland in the mid-9th century translating a precious manuscript entitled *Elements of Latin Grammar* by the scholar, Priscianus Caesariensis (aka Priscian) into (what is now called) Old Irish. The original learned document had been composed some 300 years previously in the 6th century in the Greek-speaking domain of Constantinople (Istanbul of today). So, way back well over a millennium ago, two countries who could be considered unusual bedfellows, Ireland on the extreme western edge of Europe and what has become modern-day Türkiye, on the eastern flank of the same continent, were linked through this intellectual endeavour of long ago. There was a connection between Ireland and Türkiye.

And now, in a very different context, our hotel host Şeymous was a living example of an offspring arising from two people of disparate nations on our planet who had come together. As Şeymous spoke, I felt we 'connected' with this young man because he was quite open with us about his 'story', having only met us the proverbial five minutes previously.

It shows how deep down, despite the apparent barriers of time, distance and difference, people have always followed that unwavering noble instinct of wanting to 'only connect'.

Later, as a quartet, we went out and dined in the open-air garden of a popular Diyarbakir restaurant and afterwards we had our dessert at a nearby *pastane*, a Turkish equivalent of a patisserie.

It wasn't going to be a late night for us as we had a 5am alarm call the next morning. We were departing from Türkiye on Friday 31st May and flying via Istanbul's brand-new international airport en route to other destinations: Feray, Suat and Rashida were flying back to London, whereas I was going to Thessaloniki via Athens. The reason for my journey – yet another pilgrimage of sorts – was the search for a long-lost film I had made in 1981 based on a story by a famous Greek literary figure and survivor of the Holocaust, the late Nina Kokkalidou-Nahmia, for the Thessaloniki Film Festival when I lived in northern Greece over 40 years ago but that, my dear friend, is a tale for another day.

*Marwanid Era: A historical period when the Marwanids, a Sunni Arab dynasty, held power in Northern Mesopotamia and Armenia for just under a century from about 990–1085. During this era, the Marwanid capital was established in the city of Amida (contemporary Diyarbakir) and the Marwanids were renowned for their support and patronage of art, culture, literature and architecture in the territory under their control.

Mervani Bridge over the River Tigris, close to Diyarbakir.

Downstream on the River Tigris from the Mervani Bridge.

View of the city walls, Diyarbakir.

Another aspect of the ancient city fortifications of Diyarbakir.

View of the city of Diyarbakir from the city walls.

A rural scene spotted from the top of the city walls, Diyarbakir.

Gardens within the city walls of Diyarbakir.

Sultan Şuca Türbesi Mausoleum, 13th century.

Distinctive minaret beside Sheikh Matar Mosque built on top of four former Roman columns.

Open courtyard with *shadirvan*, Great Mosque, Diyarbakir.

Hotel on the site of a caravserai, Diyarbakir.

Firin-Ci Restaurant, set within a former hamam.

Author pictured in the courtyard of the Sülüklü (leech) Han.

Peanuts for sale.

Love in a shop window, Diyarbakir.

Water source in the grounds of Diyarbakir Museum.

Sign for Diyarbakir Museum – note use of three languages: Kurdish, Turkish and English.

Jar of baked clay, Late Bronze Age 1,550–1,200 BCE, Diyarbakir Museum.

Obsidian – volcanic glass – on display at the Diyarbakir Museum.

Illustration of Al-Jazari device, Diyarbakir Museum.

Artuqids Arch, built 1206–07, serves as the entrance to Diyarbakir Museum.

The Church of St George, Roman Era, 3rd century CE – open to the elements.

Enclosed area of the Diyarbakir Museum.

TWO POEMS IN CELEBRATION

Kalamar* – Winter Sky

A winter's sky low overhead
metallic-tufted clouds
hovering with intent
above a wind-tossed sea
washed bluegrey
rippling deep relentless
in liquid movement
as white-topped waves
thunderous in their embrace
of the rocky Lycian shore
mark the softhard join
between water and land
recalling tempests of long ago
with seaborne breezes
harking back to ancient legends and omens
of nature's glorygriefed reign
forever and ever
in this beloved idyll of Kalamar

And talking of the journey we, the quartet, undertook, here is a final verse in celebration at the end of our travels:

Let us remember the enchantment
of our togetherness in Northern Mesopotamia
such wonderment on our journey
in history, through history and about history
so much to learn about life's voyage we all undertake.

---

*Kalamar

Refers to a bay within walking distance of Kalkan where the trip started; *kalamar* means squid in Turkish.

At the heart of this book is a deeply personal journey. My trip through Northern Mesopotamia (contemporary south-east Türkiye) unleashed a torrent of creative energy, fed by experiences from my entire life.

To understand my perspective, it's crucial to grasp the complex and often thorny concept of identity and roots. Blessed (and challenged) by my British and Irish heritage, I am influenced by both Anglo-Saxon and Celtic cultures, intertwined with Protestant and Catholic traditions.

With this in mind, I present a poem that delves into my mixed-heritage origins, capturing the extremes of conflict and reconciliation, and everything in between. This poem reflects the theme of duality that has played a major role in my life.

My hope is that this book inspires people to overcome differences, to let go of the need to dominate, and to embrace harmonious co-existence.

Where Do I Live Within Myself?

Where do I go –
a child of empire
and
rebellion?

How do I live –
like a conqueror
or,
the conquered?

How should I speak –
in the hushed undertones of the dispossessed
or,
in confident colonial cadences?

Which catechism of history
do I believe in –
the Celtic
or,
the Anglo-Saxon?

Who should I love more –
the British Protestant
landowner father,
son of the Ulster Plantation,
or,
the Irish Catholic landless mother,
daughter of the dispossessed,
or both the same?

What shall I value –
the metalled might of the foreign body victorious shot through with epic tales in
shiny armour,
or,
the longlasting native survivor of ancient myths cloaked in metaphor?

Where is my true allegiance –
with the victor
or,
the vanquished?

Where is my home –
Irish in Britain
or,
British in Ireland?

Which paper should I read –
the Irish Times
or,
the London Times?

What fateful tune is borne on bitter winds from a great divide –
the 'Londonderry Air'
or,
'Danny Boy'?

Which tv and radio do I trust –
RTE
or,
the BBC?

What is my culture –
Magna Carta,
Canterbury Tales
King James Bible,
On the Origin of Species
Oxford English Dictionary
or,
Brehon Laws,
The Táin
Book of Kells
Dublin Institute of Advanced Studies
De Bhaldraithe Irish dictionary

What is my religion –
Protestant, while also being RC
or,
Catholic, while also being CofI?

Who will I root for on the sports field –
Ireland's trinityed green shamrock
or,
England and the crimson cross of St George?

What should my accent be –
Irish
or,
British,
or Anglo-Irish?

What is my first language –
Gaelige
or,
English?

When I talk, do I default to Irishspeak and say,
'he's a face on him like a bulldog chewing a wasp'
or,
does Britishspeak trot off the tongue, with me uttering
'he has a face like a smacked arse'?

What are my calendar reference points –
1066, Battle of Hastings,
1690, Battle of the Boyne,
1940, Battle of Britain,
or,
1014, Battle of Clontarf,
1690, Battle of the Boyne,
1916, Easter Rising?

As a youngster, which label on my clothing and footwear did I look out for –
British made St Michael
or,
made in Ireland St Bernard?

What national anthem do I know off by heart,
'God Save The King',
or,
'Amhráin na bhFiann',
or, neither?

When I bleed,
is my blood
of an Irishman or an Englishman,
or, is it just red?

Should I practice Protestant birth control – the pill,
or,
Catholic birth control – coitus interruptus?

What is my soul –
Celtic, Catholic, Brave Defender of an ancient land
or,
Anglo-Saxon, Protestant, Courageous Conqueror from an ancient land?

What is my passported nationality –
Irish
or,
British,
or, perhaps both?

Where do I tilt my compass in search of harmony –
to the past,
or,
to horizons different?

But,
but there remains always
that devilfilled dilemma –
what is my true inner self,
and,
and, is reconciliation possible?

And since we started out with some quotations apt for the exploratory journey undertaken, by way of conclusion, let us touch on the following from a fellow Irishman:

There is another world, but it is in this one.
W.B. Yeats, *The Celtic Twilight,* 1893

EPILOGUE

Shortly after four o'clock in the morning of Monday 6th February 2023, a devastating earthquake struck south-east Türkiye and neighbouring Syria. According to the USGS (United States Geological Service), it measured 7.8 on the Richter scale. There then followed a series of aftershocks of varying degrees which added significantly to the death toll and widespread devastation.

Saddest of all is the tragedy of so many killed, injured and rendered homeless. Officially, some 53,000 people are believed to have perished, though unofficial estimates put the death toll much higher. Many were recorded as missing. It was the worst earthquake to strike Türkiye since 1939.

It had been reported that 80 per cent of the buildings in the city of Antakya, for example (which we had visited during our journey through Northern Mesopotamia) had been destroyed or so badly damaged that the only option was to rebuild. A heritage site we had been to, dating back to the 2nd century BCE, was Gaziantep Castle, which had been extensively damaged. Other cities, towns and villages elsewhere in this widespread area similarly affected will require serious attention and finance to restore the infrastructure to its pre-earthquake level of existence and operation. It will be a mammoth task.

In addition to the big picture of this horrendous event being triggered by the unstable geological tension where the Anatolian, Eurasian, African and Arabian tectonic plates collide, there was the personal perspective. Within hours of the earthquake, I was able to make contact with our tour guide Murad and to my immense relief he confirmed both he and his family were safe and well. In a later conversation though, he said that when the earthquake struck, he looked into the eyes of his wife and children and they thought they were living their last moments. "The two minutes of the earth shaking seemed like hours," Murad said. "You also realise how much you love your family," he added. Fortunately, they survived but Murad does recall hearing people trapped in the rubble of their homes in the days after the earthquake screaming out for help. But no rescue was forthcoming and those voices went quiet after a while.

But despite the overwhelming pain of tragedy, humanity did prevail as local communities came together to help each other. Hotels, restaurants and shops still standing, for instance, took immediate action offering shelter and food without charge to those who had been left with nothing more than the clothes they had on when the earthquake struck. Murad and others sprang into action and opened up a soup kitchen in Şanlıurfa (Urfa) where they helped many now destitute. Murad told me of countless shell-shocked individuals who showed up at his soup kitchen revealing they had lost entire families.

Turkish President Recep Tayyip Erdogan has admitted to 'shortcomings' in the state's response to the earthquakes but insisted the size of the affected areas and harsh winter conditions meant it was 'not possible to be prepared for such a disaster'. Turkish authorities say about 13.5 million people have been affected in an area roughly the size of Britain.

The Turkish minister of justice, Bekir Bozdag, has stated that an investigation would be launched into the collapsed buildings to identify and hold accountable everyone who had played a part.

Al Jazeera, 15th February 2023

However, some argue that widespread corruption in the construction sector and inadequate enforcement of regulations aimed at ensuring buildings are earthquake-resistant have not adequately prepared the country to deal with such catastrophic events.

Erdogan also said that the government is working hard to keep its promises to the nation, adding: "We will continue these efforts until we build and revitalize our cities." Anadolu Ajansi, 6th February 2024

A rebuilding programme is underway but at the time of writing, many people are still living in tents and former cargo containers made habitable. While a process of recovery is currently in progress, there is also the question of trauma. Psychological scars will remain for years. In addition to physical and other needs, adults and children will require continued access to appropriate counselling and support for the foreseeable future.

In addition, there is now the question of preparedness for the next 'big one' where it is feared the enormous metropolis of Istanbul with a population of 15 million people could be victim to a similar cataclysm. As a means of safeguarding against the inevitable, the prime example of Japan being 'earthquake-resilient' is receiving close attention in order to prevent or mitigate against such disasters resulting in a high level of casualties and destruction.

Earthquake-ravaged buildings in the city of Adıyaman, Adıyaman province in the south-east of Türkiye.

People left homeless from the earthquake of February 2023, in the city of Adıyaman, Adıyaman province in the south-east of Türkiye.

ENDNOTES

1. www.whitmanarchive.org/published/LG/figures/ppp.00707.387.jpg
2. According to the website www.archiqoo.com/sites/Türkiye.php
3. For further information on the Delikkemer Aqueduct, please see www.romanaqueducts.info/aquasite/patara/index.html
4. www.archaeology-world.com/the-ancient-vespasianus-titus-tunnel-of-Türkiye
5. en.wikipedia.org/wiki/Cradle_of_civilization
6. Murad was absolutely right as upon doing my research for this book, I came across the following information: Zeev Barkan on www.star-of-david.blogspot.com/2015/02/the-star-of-david-as-archaeological.html
7. www.ling-app.com/ur/urdu-numbers-and-counting
8. www.sanskritwisdom.com/sanskrit-vocabulary/numbers-in-sanskrit
9. en.wikipedia.org/wiki/Hittite_language
10. www.hurriyetdailynews.com/eu-envoy-to-turkey-visits-famed-gobeklitepe-site-165067
11. en.wikipedia.org/wiki/Cave_painting
12. www.jewishvirtuallibrary.org/euphrates
13. www.funtranslations.com/babylonian
14. en.wikipedia.org/wiki/List_of_world_folk-epics
15. en.wikipedia.org/wiki/Umayyad_Caliphate
16. www.text.npr.org/s.php?sId=858605788
17. www.thenationalnews.com/mena/iraq/2021/12/07/ancient-gilgamesh-tablet-returned-to-iraqi-national-museum
18. en.wikipedia.org/wiki/Carrowkeel_Megalithic_Cemetery
19. www.spectator.co.uk/article/does-an-unknown-extraordinarily-ancient-civilisation-lie-buried-under-eastern-Türkiye
20. www.instagram.com/reel/CnEvR3hKWm_/?igshid=MDJmNzVkMjY=
21. www.instagram.com/p/CsdZU5kJhQl
22. www.academia.edu/8030198/Karahan_Tepe_G%C3%B6bekli_Tepes_Sister_Site_Another_Temple_of_the_Stars
23. www. funtranslations.com/babylonian
24. www.metmuseum.org/art/collection/search/449534
25. www. en.wikipedia.org/wiki/Ismail_al-Jazari

Further reading on the earthquake:

www.aljazeera.com/news/2023/2/15/turkey-earthquake-how-are-people-reacting-to-state-response
www.aa.com.tr/en/turkiye/turkiye-remembers-feb-6-earthquake-victims/3128724
www.aljazeera.com/news/2024/2/5/a-year-on-from-turkeys-quake-disaster-the-trauma-haunts-survivors
www.who.int/europe/news-room/spotlight/turkiye-earthquakes-1-year-on
news.un.org/en/story/2024/02/1146262
www.usgs.gov/news/featured-story/m78-and-m75-kahramanmaras-earthquake-sequence-near-nurdagi-turkey-turkiye
www.nationalgeographic.com/environment/article/japan-earthquakes-resilient-architecture-disaster-preparedness

BIBLIOGRAPHY

Akkermans, Peter M.M.G. and Schwartz, Glenn M., *The Archaeology of Syria: From Complex Hunter-Gatherers to Early Urban Societies (c. 16,000–300 BC)* (Cambridge World Archaeology), Cambridge University Press, 2003

Akkermans, Peter M.M.G. and McMahon, Gregory (eds.), *The Oxford Handbook of Ancient Anatolia 10,000–323 BCE*, Oxford University Press, 2011

Al-Jazari, Ismail, *Book of Knowledge of Ingenious Mechanical Devices*, translated by Donald R. Hill, Springer, 1206 and 1974

Aurelius, Marcus, *Meditations*, 2nd century CE

Bertram, Stephen, *Life In Ancient Mesopotamia*, Oxford University Press, 2003

Bible, The, Cambridge University Press, 1932

Binici, Elif (interviewer), *Daily Sabah* Economy Editor, Elif Binici in conversation with Gaziantep Mayor Fatma Şahin, March 2018

Barkan, Zeev, 'The Star of David as Archaeological Artifact', *Jewish Studies Quarterly*, 2015

Cameron, Averil and Greatrex, Geoffrey (eds.), *De Bello Persico (The Persian Wars)* by Procopius of Caeserea, 6th century CE, translation, with introduction and notes, Cambridge University Press, 2022

Chahin, M., *The Kingdom of Armenia – a history*, Curzon Caucasus World, 2007

Christensen, Lars Bo (trans.), *Book of Changes – The Original Core of the I Ching*, Kindle Edition, 2016

Clow, Kate, *The Lycian Way*, Upcountry, 2009

Cohen, H. Floris, *How Modern Science Came Into The World*, Amsterdam University Press, 2012

Coleman, Graham and Jinpa, Thupten (trans.), *The Tibetan Book of the Dead*, Kindle Edition, 2006

Collins, Andrew and Hancock, Graham, *Göbekli Tepe Genesis of the Gods: The Temple of the Watchers and the Discovery of Eden*, Bear and Company, 2014

Crawford, Harriet, *Sumer and the Sumerians*, 2nd edition, Cambridge University Press, 2004

Croke, Brian and Crow, James, 'Procopius and Dara', *The Journal of Roman Studies,* 1983, Vol. 73, pp. 143–159

Dalley, Stephanie, *Myths From Mesopotamia: Creation, the Flood, Gilgamesh and Others*, Oxford World Classics, 2008

Dankoff, Robert & Kim, Sooyong (ed. and trans.), *An Ottoman Traveller – Selections for the Book of Travels of Evliya Çelebi*, Eland, 2010

Dawood, N.J. (trans.), The Koran, Penguin Classics, 2003

De Bhaldraithe, English-Irish Dictionary, An Gúm Foras na Gaeilge, 2023

Dewing, H.B. (trans.), *De Aedificiis (Buildings)* by Procopius of Caeserea, 6th century CE, William Heinemann, 1940

Diyarbakir City Museum, Diyarbakir

Easwaran, Eknath (trans.), The Bhagavad Gita, 2011

Edwards, I.E.S., Gadd, C.J., Hammond, N.G.L., *Cambridge Ancient History* Vol 1 Part 1, Cambridge University Press, 1970

Ferguson, Margaret, et al., *The Norton Anthology of Poetry*, 4th edition, W.W. Norton & Company, 1996

Finkel, Irving and Taylor, Jonathan, *Cuneiform*, British Museum, 2015

Fitzgerald Johnson, Scott (ed.), *Oxford Handbook of Late Antiquity*, Oxford University Press, 2012

Forster, E.M., *Howard's End*, Penguin Classics, 2000

Freely, John, *The Western Shores of Türkiye*, Tauris Parke, 2008

Gadd, C.J., *The Highways of Asia Minor*, British School at Athens, 1956

Harbison, Peter, *Pre-Christian Ireland: From the First Settlers to the Early Celts* (Ancient Peoples and Places), Thames and Hudson, 1988

Hatay Archaeological Museum, Antakya

Hensey, Robert, Meehan, Padraig, Dowd, Marion, Moore, Sam, *A Century of Archaeology – Historical Excavation and Modern Research at the Carrowkeel Passage Tombs, County Sligo*, proceedings of the Royal Irish Academy, vol. 114C, 2014

Holland, Charles Hepworth and Sanders, Ian S. (eds.), *The Geology of Ireland*, 2nd Edition, Dunedin Academic Press, 2009

Holland, Charles Hepworth, *The Idea of Time*, John Wiley and Sons, 1999

Holland, Tom (trans.), *The Histories* by Herodotus, 5th century BCE, Penguin Classics, 2013

Holmes, Arthur, *Principles of Physical Geology*, 1971

Kassabova, Kapka, *Border*, Granta, 2017

Kinoshita, Sharon (trans.), *The Description of the World* by Marco Polo, Hackett Publishing, 2016

Kramer, Samuel Noah, *The Sumerians: Their History, Culture, and Character*, University of Chicago Press, 1971

Kramer, Samuel Noah, *Sumerian Mythology*, revised edition, University of Pennsylvania Press, 1972, originally published 1944

Larrington, Carolyne (trans.), *The Poetic Edda*, Oxford World's Classics, 2014

Lawall, Sarah Ph.D. et al. (ed.), *The Norton Anthology of World Literature*, Vol. A: Beginnings to A.D. 100 (CE), 2nd edition, W.W. Norton and Company, 2003

Lawall, Sarah Ph.D. et al., (ed.), *The Norton Anthology of World Literature*, Vol. B: Beginnings to 100–1500 (CE), 2nd edition, W.W. Norton and Company, 2003

Lawrence, T.E., The Diary of 1911, Monday, July 17, from *The Essential T.E Lawrence*, Jonathan Cape, 1951

Mackintosh-Smith, Tim (ed.), *The Travels of Ibn Battuta*, Macmillan, 2003

Marcellinus, Ammianus, *Res Gestae*, translated by Walter Hamilton, Penguin Classics, 4th century CE and 2004

Mardin Museum, Mardin

McQueen, J.G., *The Hittites and their Contemporaries in Asia Minor* (Ancient Peoples and Places), Thames & Hudson, 1986

Mellaart, James, *The Archaeology of Ancient Türkiye*, Bodley Head Archaeology, 1978

Mieroop, Marc Van De, *A History of the Ancient Near East ca. 3,000–323 BC*, Blackwell Publishing, 2007

Moody, T.W. and Martin, F.X., *The Course of Irish History*, Mercier Press, 2001

Murphy, Anthony, *Newgrange: Monument to Immortality*, The Liffey Press, 2012

Oppenheim, A. Leo, *Ancient Mesopotamia – a portrait of a dead civilization*, Chicago University Press, 1997

O'Rahilly, T.F., *Early Irish History and Mythology*, Dublin Institute of Advanced Studies, 1964

Pamuk, Orhan, *The Museum of Innocence*, 2006

Pinch, Geraldine, *Egyptian Mythology: A Guide to the Gods, Goddesses, and Traditions of Ancient Egypt*, Kindle Edition, 2022

Plath, Sylvia, *The Bell Jar*, Faber & Faber, 2001

Plato, *Republic*, translated by Robin Waterfield, Oxford University Press, 1993

Plato, *The Symposium*, translated by Benjamin Jowett, Kindle Edition, 2021

Radner, Karen and Robson, Eleanor (eds.), *The Oxford Handbook of Cuneiform Culture*, Oxford University Press, 2020

Roller, Duane W. (trans.), *Geography* by Strabo, Cambridge University Press, 2020

Sayce, Archibald Henry, *An Elementary Grammar with Full Syllabary and Progressive Reading Book, of The Assyrian Language in The Cuneiform Type*, Cambridge University Press, 2014, originally published 1875

Schmidt, Klaus et al., 'The role of cult and feasting in the emergence of Neolithic communities. New evidence from Göbeklitepe, south-eastern Türkiye', *Antiquity* by Cambridge University Press, 2012

Shafak, Elif, *How To Stay Sane In An Age Of Division*, 2020

Shakespeare, William, *The Complete Works*, Collins, 1987

Shonagon, Sei, *The Pillow Book*, translated by Meredith McKinney, Penguin Classics, Kindle Edition, 2006

Steadman, Sharon R. and McMahon, Gregory (eds.), *The Oxford Handbook of Ancient Anatolia 10,000–323 BCE*, Oxford University Press, 2011

Sweatman, Martin, *Göbeklitepe: Prehistory Decoded*, Troubador, 2018

Taylor, Richard C., Adamson, Peter (eds.), *The Cambridge Companion to Arabic Philosophy*, Cambridge University Press, 2011

Teonge, Henry, Diary by Reverend Henry Teonge, first published 1825, edited with the addition of an Introduction and Notes by G.E. Manwaring, 1927

Van De Mieroop, Marc, *A History of the Ancient Near East ca. 3,000–323 BC*, Blackwell Publishing, 2007

Wellhausen, Julius, *The Arab Kingdom and Its Fall*, Wellhausen Press, 2008

Williams, David G., *Eastern Türkiye, A Guide and History*, Tauris Parke, 2008

Yeats, W.B., *The Second Coming*, 1919

Yeats, W.B., *The Collected Works of W.B. Yeats*, Pergamon Media, Kindle edition, 2015

Yule, Henry, Cordier, Henri (eds.), *The Travels of Marco Polo, The Complete Yule-Cordier Edition*, Dover, 1993

Zeugma Mosaic Museum, Sanliurfa

INDEX

Published in 2024 by Unicorn,
an imprint of Unicorn Publishing Group, Charleston Studio, Meadow Business Centre, Lewes BN8 5RW
www.unicornpublishing.org

Text and photographs © Nicholas Mackey
except for the following images: p. 135 courtesy of Wikimedia Commons; pp. 138, 140 Justin Mackey;
p. 195 The Metropolitan Museum of Modern Art, Rogers Fund, 1938; pp. 240–42 Murad Sunbul
Maps © Battlefield Design

ISBN 978-1-916846-28-9
10 9 8 7 6 5 4 3 2 1

Printed in Türkiye by Fine Tone Ltd

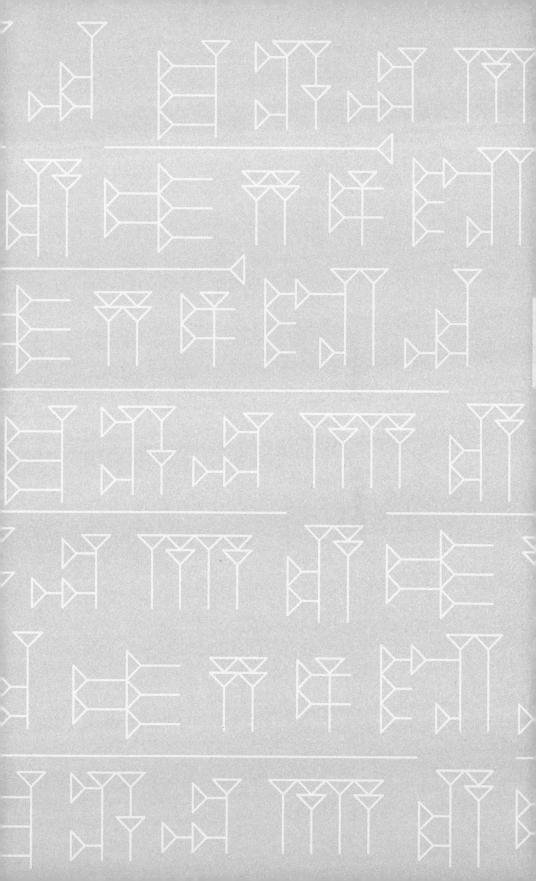